A Bittersweet Land

GENERATIONS

A History of Canada's Peoples

A Bittersweet Land

The Dutch Experience in Canada, 1890-1980

Herman Ganzevoort

Published by McClelland and Stewart in association
with the Multiculturalism Program,
Department of the Secretary of State
and the Canadian Government Publishing Centre,
Supply and Services, Canada.

Catalogue No. Ci44-13/1988E

Canadian Cataloguing in Publication Data
Ganzevoort, H., 1942–
  A bittersweet land

(Generations, a history of Canada's peoples)
Co-published by the Multiculturalism Directorate.
Bibliography: p.
Includes index.
ISBN 0-7710-3272-2

1. Dutch Canadians – History. I. Canada.
Multiculturalism Directorate. II. Title.
III. Series.

FC106.D9G36 1988   971′.0043931   C87-095159-9
F1035.D8G36 1988

Printed and bound in Canada

McClelland and Stewart
The Canadian Publishers
481 University Avenue
Toronto, Ontario
M5G 2E9

Contents

Editors' Introduction / *vi*

Preface / *1*

Part One: The Ripple, 1890-1918
ONE: The Decision to Emigrate / *5*
TWO: The Early Settlers / *17*

Part Two: The Wave, 1918-1939
THREE: Between the Wars: Why They Came / *35*
FOUR: Settling In / *45*

Part Three: The Flood and Ebb, 1939-1980
FIVE: The Second World War and Its Aftermath / *61*
SIX: On to Canada! / *74*
SEVEN: Problems of Adjustment / *84*
EIGHT: The Changing Fifties and Sixties / *93*
NINE: The Community Today / *114*

Bibliography / *129*
Index / *131*

Editors' Introduction

Canadians, like many other people, have recently been changing their attitude toward the ethnic dimension in society. Instead of thinking of the many distinctive heritages and identities to be found among them as constituting a problem, though one that time would solve, they have begun to recognize the ethnic diversity of their country as a rich resource. They have begun to take pride in the fact that people have come and are coming here from all parts of the world, bringing with them varied outlooks, knowledge, skills, and traditions, to the great benefit of all.

It is for this reason that Book IV of the *Report of the Royal Commission on Bilingualism and Biculturalism* dealt with the cultural contributions of the ethnic groups other than the British, the French, and the Native peoples to Canada, and that the federal government in its response to Book IV announced that the Citizenship Branch of the Department of the Secretary of State would commission "histories specifically directed to the background, contributions and problems of various cultural groups in Canada." This series presents the histories that have resulted from that mandate. Although commissioned by the government, they are not intended as definitive or official, but rather as the efforts of scholars to bring together much of what is known about the ethnic groups studied, to indicate what remains to be learned, and thus to stimulate further research concerning the ethnic dimension in Canadian society. The histories are to be objective, analytical, and readable, and directed toward the general reading public, as well as students at the senior high school and the college and university levels, and teachers in the elementary schools.

Most Canadians belong to an ethnic group, since to do so is simply to have "a sense of identity rooted in a common origin . . . whether this common origin is real or imaginary."[1] The Native peoples, the British and French (referred to as charter groups because they were the first Europeans to take possession of the land), the groups such as the Germans and Dutch who have been established in Canada for over a hundred years, and those who began to arrive only yesterday all have traditions and values they cherish and that now are part of the cultural riches Canadians share. The groups vary widely in numbers, geographical location and distribution, and degree of social and economic power. The stories of their struggles, failures, and triumphs will be told in this series.

As the Royal Commission on Bilingualism and Biculturalism pointed out, this sense of ethnic origin or identity "is much keener in certain individuals than in others."[2] In contemporary Canadian society, with the increasing number of intermarriages across ethnic lines, and hence the growing diversity of people's ancestors, many are coming to identify themselves simply as Canadian, without reference to their ancestral origins. In focusing on the ethnic dimension of Canadian society, past and present, the series does not assume that everyone should be categorized into one particular group, or that ethnicity is always the most important dimension of people's lives. It is, however, one dimension that needs examination if we are to understand fully the contours and nature of Canadian society and identity.

Professional Canadian historians have in the past emphasized political and economic history, and since the country's economic and political institutions have been controlled largely by people of British and French origin, the role of those of other origins in the development of Canada has been neglected. Also, Canadian historians in the past have been almost exclusively of British and French origin and have lacked the interest and the linguistic skills necessary to explore the history of other ethnic groups. Indeed, there has rarely even been an examination of the part played by specifically British – or, better, specifically English, Irish, Scottish, and Welsh – traditions and values in Canadian development because of the lack of recognition of pluralism in the society. The part played by French traditions and values, and particular varieties of French traditions and values, has for a number of reasons been more carefully scrutinized.

This series is an indication of growing interest in Canadian social history, which includes immigration and ethnic history. This may partially be a reflection of an increasing number of scholars whose origins and ethnic identities are other than British or French. Because such trends are recent, many of the authors of the histories in this series have not had a large body of published writing to work from. It is true that some histories have already been written of particular groups other than the British and French; but these have often been characterized by filiopietism, a narrow perspective, and a dearth of scholarly analysis.

Despite the scarcity of secondary sources, the authors have been asked to be as comprehensive as possible and to give balanced coverage to a number of themes: historical background, settlement patterns, ethnic identity and assimilation, ethnic associations, population trends, religion, values, occupations and social class, the family, the ethnic press, language patterns, political behaviour, education, inter-ethnic relations, the arts, and recreation. They have also been asked to give a sense of the way the group differs in various parts of the country. Finally, they have been asked to give, as much as possible, an insider's view of what the immigrant and ethnic experiences were like at different periods of time, but yet at the same time to be as objective as possible and not simply to present the group as it sees itself or as it would like to be seen.

The authors have thus been faced with a herculean task. To the extent that they have succeeded, they provide us with new glimpses into many aspects of Canadian society of the past and the present. To the extent that they have fallen short of their goal, they challenge other historians, sociologists, and social anthropologists to continue the work begun here.

Jean Burnet
Howard Palmer

1   *Report of the Royal Commission on Bilingualism and Biculturalism.*
2   *Ibid.*, Paragraph 8.

Preface

People of Dutch birth or origin have had some connection with Canada since the days of the early French fur traders, but they played no significant role as an ethnic group in Canada's historical development until the last decades of the nineteenth century. Researching the story of the Dutch in Canada immediately presented some problems. In the early 1970's very little had been written about them and nothing had been collected or catalogued. There were no manuscript collections, no microfilm archival holdings; in fact, little existed except an occasional reference or paper on some particular individual or group that had piqued the interest of a researcher. Simply gathering the facts and figures, documents, government papers, and all the other minutiae promised to be a formidable task. Since that time, individuals and groups have begun successfully to gather the evidence and, slowly, the history of the Dutch in Canada has begun to emerge.

As the evidence was collected, it became apparent that the Dutch have played an important role in North American history since the early 1600's. However, their contact was originally limited to the colony of New Netherlands, the present-day state of New York, and its neighbours and later to the pre-revolutionary Thirteen Colonies. The American Revolution produced the first significant contact of the Dutch with Canada when Loyalists of Dutch-American origin entered the British North American colonies seeking asylum. Although I considered the possibility of beginning the history at this point, a number of factors militated against it. By 1783 Dutch Americans were almost fully integrated into the culture of the American colonies. Although some still retained the Dutch language, they also spoke English. They shared in the commonly held values of their time and culture. They were, as were many of their fellow Loyalists, strangers to Canada but not strangers in it. While their children and their future progeny would continue to regard themselves as being of Dutch origin, this was to have no significance except as some kind of positive social identifier.

These Dutch-American Loyalists were joined in their flight to Canada by Mennonites and other American Anabaptists of German origin whose pacifism had brought them into disfavour with the American revolutionaries. Identifying themselves as "Deutsch" (commonly corrupted into Dutch), or perhaps even tracing their origins back to the Netherlands and their founder Menno Simons, their arrival made any clear identification of a Dutch-Canadian community almost impossible. Their religion did distinguish them from their Dutch-American compatriots, who were either members of the various American churches or belonged to the Dutch Reformed Church of America, which would soon wither in Canada's religious diversity. But to the general society, all were regarded as Dutch.

Although a few Dutchmen would make their way to Canada, in the years following the American Revolution, the great mass of the migration that left the Netherlands beginning in the 1840's streamed into the new frontier land of the American Midwest and West. Not until the American frontier closed in the late 1880's and early 1890's would the immigrant waves be redirected to the Canadian West, taking along with them second-generation Dutch Americans. It is at that moment that the Dutch become a truly identifiable ethnic minority in Canada and their story can begin.

Yet even this migration presents the historian with some serious problems. Dutch Americans and immigrants from the Netherlands who entered through the United States cannot be easily distinguished from the great mass of other immigrants. The statistics kept by the Canadian government before 1918 can only be charitably categorized as inconsistent and unhelpful. Lack of consistency in gathering data and variable ethnic designations such as "Belgian-Dutch" create confusions which, unfortunately, are not clarified by the unreliable Dutch statistics.

Census material clouds the issue further: for a considerable period of time ethnicity was determined not by birthplace or parents' birthplace but by the nationality of one's forefathers. The problem such vague characterization of ethnicity can present is poignantly demonstrated by the census of 1921, which indicates that the Dutch-Canadian population had doubled in the previous decade, from 55,961 in 1911 to 117,505 in 1921. The answer to this impossible growth lies in the realization that Mennonites who had registered their ancestry as German in 1911 listed it as Dutch in 1921, to avoid the stigma of German nationality during and after World War I. The statistics arrived at in this work are based on the best figures available from Dutch, Canadian, and American sources, but they must be characterized as educated guesses.

A comment should also be made on the sources. Immigration files and material were available from both Canadian and Dutch sources. Officials and workers in the emigration and immigration fields, past and present, were available for interviews and consultation. Where those sources have been utilized they have been directly referred to by name and identified.

Most important to this work have been the personal interviews the immigrants and their children have given to me. Over the more than fifteen years I have spent researching the Dutch in Canada, I have talked to thousands of people who had their own stories to share. Whether these occasions were formal interviews, complete with recorder and notebook, or simple chats over coffee, they all helped to build a strong sense and understanding of the human dimension of the migration. Numbers and groups acquired faces and personal histories: policies and proclamations affected real men, women, and children. Their stories, like those of immigrants from other countries, were often commonplace and similar, but they were their stories. Only with their help could this history have been written, because their experiences make up this work. From Newfoundland to the Queen Charlotte Islands they have shared their lives with me, and this book is dedicated to them. Though most of them remain anonymous and unidentified in the footnotes, this book records their story and my thanks.

There are others who have had a direct and important role to play in the completion of this history. The Multiculturalism Directorate of the Secretary of State made this financially possible, as did the Canadian government's commitment to a multicultural Canada. R. Craig Brown helped me begin the long journey of rediscovery. The Netherlands Emigration Service found the documents and have continued to support this work. *Wereld Contact* gave of its time and energy and money to realize the dream. Those two stalwart friends, John Houkes and Gerritt Stallinga, opened the doors and their hearts and never said no. The editors advised and contributed; friends, acquaintances, and family asked when it would be done. Last, but not least, my wife, Karen Fry, with infinite patience and love, convinced me it could be done. To all of them go thanks for a job well done.

This is a history about the Dutch in Canada written by a Dutch Canadian. It is a personal testimony to the strengths and weakness of those who ventured to a new land and came to love it. It is a history of ordinary people, written for ordinary people. There are few heroes and fewer villains, simply people who measured up to the ultimate challenge of survival. I hope I have done as much.

H.G.
January, 1988

PART ONE

The Ripple, 1890–1918

ONE

The Decision to Emigrate

The last decade of the nineteenth century found the Netherlands in the midst of a revolution, although there were no troops in the streets or milling crowds at barricades chanting for change. The previous thirty years had transformed a predominantly rural and agricultural society into an urban industrial one. The changes had been immense, rapid, and at times disturbing. The five million citizens of this small country were experiencing the traumatic changes of the industrial age.

All of life seemed to have been altered, and to many it seemed for the better: who could deny "progress" when its accomplishments were to be seen everywhere? Networks of train tracks criss-crossed the countryside linking even the smallest towns in the far corners of the provinces. Electricity and telegraph, telephone and postal delivery, expanding canal service and booming industries were signs of a flourishing and developing economy. Every year the nation's exports increased; every year the cities grew a little larger to accommodate the growing numbers of workers. Even the less material aspects of national life were stimulated by this revolution, as the fine arts, theatre, architecture, and literature experienced an unexpected flowering.

True, there were problems. There were economic disparities between classes of people, poverty and crime, prostitution and alcoholism, industrial pollution and exploitation. But these, after all, were solvable problems, ones that could be approached rationally and reasonably. Most believed that, given time and planning, even mankind's age-old scourges could be eliminated and a new and better society created. Optimism was not simply a slogan, it was a belief, backed by science and reason, and the progress of the changing society seemed to support and encourage that belief.

Even the problems of the agricultural sector had seemed to suggest that some kind of rational solution could be applied. The world depression, which had begun in 1873, rapidly impinged on all economic sectors of the Western trading nations, but its effects were most acutely felt by the agriculturalists. By 1878 Dutch farmers were suffering from the restrictive trade policies of Germany and England, which seriously limited their exports of cattle, margarine, and dairy products. They found themselves in competition with massive imports of cheap American grain, which brought about an alarming decline in the prices of their home-grown products. Restrictions by other European trading partners reduced the prices of beans, peas, potatoes, sugar beets, and meat and dairy products. The cost of production was simply too high to make their produce competitive.

An investigation by the Dutch government in 1880 had pointed out some very serious shortcomings. Dutch agriculture was behind the times. Techniques, marketing systems, education, and products were not adequate for the existing markets and needed to be revamped. The processes of rationalization and organization that had worked so successfully in the industrial sector needed to be applied here. The rapid implementation of these recommendations did much to modernize Dutch agriculture and re-establish it as the firm base of the Dutch economy.

The changes brought about by these reforms were soon evident. New methods of production such as greenhouse cultivation of vegetables and flowers were quickly accepted. The introduction of artificial fertilizers to increase yield on small acreages soon brought costs down. The development of the co-operative movement made rapid strides in reorganizing marketing, buying, and distribution for the farmers. By the mid-1890's, eggs, cheese, butter, fruit, vegetables, and flowers were becoming important assets to the Dutch economy.

The co-operative movement even extended into the banking area with the formation first of farmers' savings and loan institutions on a local level, then the establishment of a national organization dedicated to extending credit and offering advice for agricultural modernization. Co-operation in the form of farmers' alliances helped bring about uniformity in production and marketing, new methods, upgrading in technique, the establishment by the government of national agricultural schools and other reforms and changes, all of which gradually ameliorated the worst effects of economic instability and changing world markets.

In any process of change there are winners and losers, and this was no exception. As urban workers became victims of rapid industrialization and sought relief in unionism, so there were those on the land who had benefited little from all the experimentation and change. In the deepest crisis years of the depression, independent farmers and farm labourers, without capital reserves, were especially disadvantaged. With prices at an all-time low, and with few opportunities for farm employment, there was a steady trek of agricultural workers into the cities of the Netherlands and the rest of industrial Europe. Germany, in particular, proved to be a haven for the unemployed.

The industrial centres of Germany and the Netherlands were, however, alien places to those who had spent their formative years in the *polders* and flat countryside of the Netherlands. Local custom, costume, and even dialect were altered in the grey uniformity of urban industrial life. In the provinces of South Holland, North Holland, and Utrecht, which were now the high industrial growth areas of the Netherlands, religious traditions, provincial attitudes, and the farmers' much vaunted independence seemed to be threatened by the new order. Not all were prepared to accept the "better way" of doing things and some came to the conclusion that there had to be an alternative to acceptance of the new lifestyle.

Those who remained on the land experienced at first hand the revolutionary changes of agricultural modernization. The introduction of labour-saving machinery turned the farm hand into a seasonal worker faced with intermittent unemployment. Even those who formed farmworker organizations and pursued a program of labour politics foresaw little prospect of real change. Small farmers with rental holdings and little capital or collateral could not hope to purchase farm machinery and fell further behind those who had access to more modern equipment.

Even farmers and farm hands who had benefited from the slow but sure rise in the value of agricultural products after 1895 found their opportunities for advancement seriously curtailed. Few farmers were able to expand their holdings and even fewer farm hands were able to begin on their own. The problem was simple: arable land was in short supply in the Netherlands and many large tracts were controlled by absentee landlords who parcelled out the land in minuscule portions to those who could pay the highest rents. The process of rehabilitating waste land was arduous and expensive and the potential acreage fell far short of demand. If industrial employment and the cities were to be shunned, if economic security and opportunity were to be grasped, there was only one frontier left – America.

It is not difficult to recreate the popular European image of the golden land. Newspapers, books, and letters of the time are full of descriptions of that mythical haven. It was a dreamlike land, vast in extent, filled with prairies, trees, mountains and Indians, farmland without end, streets paved with gold, immense cities peopled by classless democrats striving for economic security. True enough, relatives sometimes wrote the unvarnished truth, but as often as not it was dismissed as applicable only to others. America meant a land of opportunity where hard work and a desire to succeed brought unimaginable rewards. No distinction was made between Canada and the United States: all North America was "Amerika" and economic bounty awaited those strong enough to seize it.

By the 1890's there was a significant Dutch presence in the United States. The old colonial settlements in New York had been displaced by immigration in the late 1840's and early 1850's to the new western frontier of Michigan and Iowa. Driven, at that time, by the economic disruption of the potato blight, political unrest, and government persecution of Calvinist dissenters, Dutch immigrants flooded into the Midwest states. Their new settlements had expanded and seeded colonies in Illinois, North Dakota, South Dakota, Montana, and Washington. The communities presented a strong attraction to Dutch agriculturalists, as they offered a place in a society well past the frontier stage. Not only farmers but shopkeepers, skilled artisans, clerks, and even professionals were welcome in the American settlements. Here the

7

Dutch language was maintained, the Calvinist church flourished, and the whole social milieu resembled the small towns of the Netherlands. The shocks of displacement, a foreign language, and loneliness, even on a homestead frontier, were cushioned by a receptive community and church. Best of all, economic opportunity and success were a realistic hope and a possibility, a possibility that no longer seemed to exist in the Netherlands.[1]

By 1890 it had become clear that the opportunities for advancement in the Dutch-American settlements, at least in the agricultural field, were diminishing. Cheap arable land became less and less available. The problems of mechanization, distribution, financing, and transportation also began to plague American farmers. Rapid expansion, the development of marginal land, overcropping, and the imposition of tariffs threatened to put many American farmers out of business. Dutch Americans were now beginning, if only tentatively, to examine the possibilities on a new frontier: the Canadian Prairies. As the agricultural frontier of the United States began to close and Canada began to advertise the virtues of the West, Canada assumed a more important part in the Dutch agriculturalist's consideration of emigration to America.[2]

For many farm people the possession of land was equated with economic stability and success. Jobs might disappear in economic depressions, homes and possessions might fall to civil strife or war, but the land was eternal and food a human necessity. If money and land were unavailable in the Netherlands and the United States, then only Canada remained as a place where one could acquire good land merely by the strength of the hands and the sweat of the brow. Emigration became, then, a speculative decision based on the belief that economic betterment would result from the move. If that decision to emigrate meant excitement, new places, and adventure, so much the better.

DUTCH EMIGRATION POLICY, 1890-1918

As interest began to grow in the possibility of emigration, many Dutch citizens looked to their government to take the lead in giving the movement some direction. What they found was a government that remained purposefully uninterested in the fate of the emigrants. The state exerted no control over the departure of its citizens beyond a legal concern for their transportation. It regulated accommodations, length of voyage, and general conditions on shipping originating in the Netherlands under the old Emigration Law of 1861. But no laws regulated the actions of agents and societies that encouraged emigration. While a commission was established in 1907 to recommend changes in the existing law in order to combat some of the worst abuses, its final report was not issued until 1917 and even then it only concerned itself with recommending changes in the transportation of emigrants and transmigrants. No controls were placed on propaganda or emigration societies.

The government's attitude is understandable, given the nature of Dutch society at the turn of the century. Filled with an optimism created by apparent advances in the industrial and agricultural sectors, it felt that any meddling would hinder the natural developmental process the society was undergoing. The government believed that false propaganda and underhanded tactics in the emigration field were self-limiting – the abuses would lead to a decline in interest that would naturally result in the survival of only the fittest and best organizations. Furthermore, nothing, it seemed to say, should disturb the work and profits of those who had a financial interest in emigration.

This laissez-faire attitude was further supported by a belief that any official pronouncements on the emigration issue might commit the government to making decisions in a controversial area in which it had no competence. It was content to support those mortgage institutions and Dutch investors who had long been interested in railway building, land speculation, and providing capital for Canadian and American farmers. Making money overseas not only benefited the Netherlands but seemed to be an apolitical and uncontentious issue.[3]

Furthermore, the government appeared to be supported in its position by the attitude of the Dutch public. Given the tremendous economic gains in society after 1895, there seemed to be no mass movement for emigration. Most were not tempted to emigrate, and those who did move often went to other European countries from which return was not only possible but expected. Many of the public and their representatives concluded that the whole issue was nothing more than the pet hobby horse of certain pressure groups, which had no real societal support, and could simply be dismissed.

THE EMIGRATION SOCIETIES

The economic circumstances that produced an interest in emigration among the Dutch farming communities stimulated the development of emigration societies and the activities of those who saw an opportunity for financial gain from the emigrant traffic. As the societies were, for the most part, conceived with altruistic motives for encouraging the movement of people from Holland, they quickly came into conflict with those who had more mercenary reasons for their activity. The period before and during the First World War set the stage not only for emigration to Canada but also for a struggle that would involve the societies in constant altercations with individuals, companies, and governments.

On February 18, 1892, the Christian Emigration Society held a meeting in the city of Utrecht to discuss the necessity of emigration. It was agreed that, given the existing bad economic conditions in the countryside of Friesland, emigration was a viable alternative to unemployment. Robert Insinger of Yorkton, Saskatchewan, the society's Canadian correspondent, was instructed to approach the Canadian Department of the Interior to see if there was a possibility of settling groups of unemployed Friesian farm labourers on free Canadian land grants.[4] The Canadian government was generally opposed to group settlement and favoured individual homesteading. It was, however, impressed by the wealth and status of the society's organizers and their willingness to lend money for transportation and settlement and offered to apply the existing bonus system to the society for the recruitment of immigrants for homesteads. Ten dollars was to be given for each adult male settler and five dollars for each wife and for each child over twelve years of age. If any member of the family over the age of eighteen took up an additional homestead, the society was to receive an extra five dollars.[5]

Believing that the bonuses would provide a sufficient immediate return for the Amsterdam bankers who were underwriting the loans for transportation and settlement, the Christian Emigration Society sent out 102 emigrants to Winnipeg and Yorkton in the spring of 1893. In the summer of that year one of the directors of the society came to Canada to make an inspection tour. He was well received by the Department of the Interior representatives and was suitably impressed by the promising conditions in Canada. The department was so enthused as to even discuss the possibility of producing propaganda material on Canada in Dutch. Dutch emigration to Canada seemed to be well under way.

By 1894, however, the enthusiasm had waned considerably. The bankers began to feel that the returns were too meagre and explored the possibility of investing their capital in land speculation around Edmonton, Alberta. The emigrants themselves were less than encouraging in their letters home. They complained about the long cold winters, poor pay, hard work, and difficulties of homesteading. As a result the society decided to postpone any plans for large-scale assisted emigration. Once again it focused on getting a land grant for a colony settlement and at the same time recruited emigrants with the financial ability to pay their own transportation costs.[6] The Canadian government declined to discuss the idea of land grants and opposed suggestions that emigrants be granted low fares and that the society agents also be granted free passage to Canada. The Canadian officials feared that the society was simply a money-making venture.

By 1897, the Christian Emigration Society had all but given up its interest in settlement in Canada. The revival of the economy in the Netherlands and increasing employment made recruitment difficult and, apparently, unnecessary. Furthermore, the emigrants appeared not to be all that trustworthy, as they had not repaid their loans to the society.[7] Any interest at all in emigration oriented itself to the United States rather than to Canada and the Canadian government was not prepared to strike a bargain that would encourage the society to change its attitude.

Although the Christian Emigration Society was one of the first organizations to enter the emigration field with avowedly philanthropic motives, it was soon followed by others. The City of Haarlem Emigration Commission provided loans for transportation and settlement in Europe or elsewhere. In 1913 this commission lent travel money to two cigar-makers who went to try their luck in Toronto.[8] Although details are not available beyond a few passing references, it can be supposed that other organizations were interested in emigration for the purposes of social relief, though none of them appear to have been very successful.

The only organization that had any considerable impact in promoting emigration was the Dutch Salvation Army. In 1907 it appointed Adjutant Frijlink to recruit emigrants; in that year an estimated 150 Dutchmen were sent to Canada from English ports. The Army's interest was primarily humanitarian in that it was dedicated to providing cheap passage and a new life in Canada for those who appeared to be victims of the economic or social malaise in their home countries.[9]

The Salvation Army classified the emigrants as to occupation and skills and attempted to place them either on farms or in their own occupations in urban areas. Employers would then remit a portion of the wages to the Army for the repayment of the passage. Unfortunately, the placements were often inadequate and emigrants were badly exploited by their employers. A severe drawback to this work was the suspicion with which it was met by emigrants who were not themselves Salvationists. Catholics, non-churched, and other Protestants regarded the Army religious principles as either dangerous or heretical. But the Salvation Army made no religious demands on those it transported, and in the end only 40 per cent of its passage loans to Dutch emigrants were repaid.[10]

This work came under some severe criticism from the Canadian government in that many Dutch immigrants to Canada had to be repatriated because of their inability to establish themselves. Furthermore, many of them settled in urban areas and competed for industrial jobs, precisely what the Canadian government did not want. The Army's financial interest in the emigration movement was also attacked in that it received a £1 bonus for each emigrant and a premium from the transportation companies for each passage. Because no accurate figures exist, it is impossible to determine how many people the Army actually aided in their emigration from the Netherlands, but it certainly equalled if not exceeded the number recruited by other organizations.

Those who supported emigration as a viable alternative to unemployment and saw it as a measure for achieving upward social and economic mobility were a small group, but a vocal one. They regarded the government's hands-off policy as an abandonment of its duty to the public. Pressure from agricultural societies, unemployment commissions, and even a few government members kept the issue of emigration before the public. Deep concern was voiced over inadequate sources of information for emigrants, the effect of uncontrolled emigration schemes on the future of the movement, and the ingenuity and deceitfulness of uncontrolled emigration agents.

To co-ordinate their activities and exert more pressure on the government, in 1913 the interested groups formed the *Nederlandse Vereniging Landverhuizing* (the Netherlands Emigration League). The NEL received the semi-official blessing of the government as it was granted a small annual subsidy of 10,000 guilders by the Ministry of Agriculture. What to this time had been a purely private movement composed of various independent emigration societies now became a semi-official organization committed to give leadership to the whole movement and to combat the illusory and false propaganda that organizations and agents were using to recruit emigrants. The two prime aims of the society were to gather accurate information on immigration lands and to attempt to halt such unwise practices as the recruitment of industrial workers for overseas farm jobs. While the government still kept its distance it had in some sense committed itself to the regulation of emigration traffic.[11]

From its inception the Netherlands Emigration League functioned mainly as an information-gathering organization. In the summer of 1913, the new director, J. Maurer, made an extensive trip to North America to gauge emigration possibilities. He was particularly disappointed by what he saw in Canada. It soon became evident to him that Dutch immigrants had not been well served by the Canadian immigration services, public or private. Placements had often been inappropriate as many farmers were interested in getting the maximum work out of an immigrant without considering the necessity to train him. The immigrant's inability to speak English and his lack of Canadian agricultural experience also hindered his advancement. Homesteading, it seemed, was a much more difficult process than envisioned and took not only immense amounts of energy but at least 320 acres and a substantial amount of capital. He noticed that far too many immigrants failed and made their way into the city to join the lines of the unemployed. He reached the inevitable conclusion that homesteading was only for those with agricultural experience and that urban labourers, clerks, and skilled tradesmen would never succeed in that venture. As a result the League became more interested in steering emigrants to possibilities on improved farms in the West or mixed farming areas in Ontario rather than to homestead lands in the Prairie provinces.[12]

The outbreak of the First World War ended any significant movement of the Dutch to foreign lands. Lack of finances curtailed the activities of the NEL and internal conflicts were indicative of the uncertainty in Dutch society about emigration. Disagreement centred on the encouragement of emigration by pamphlet and speeches. The final consensus was that prospective emigrants should not be recruited by such methods but simply should be provided with accurate information. Encouragement of emigration was avoided because a fear began to grow that a great exodus might occur at the end of the war and that such a loss of people would damage the industrial potential of the nation. The League also feared that a significant number of women would go to America as domestics and that many men would leave for Germany as labourers. Thus, emigration encouragement was regarded as a dangerous practice in a nation needing all of its manpower for the future economic revival.[13]

THE AGENTS

The economic circumstances that gave rise to an interest in emigration and stimulated the development of emigration societies also produced the emigration agent. Alternately cursed and praised, hailed as the saviour or condemned as a "judas-goat," he was a man seldom ignored either by the emigrants or the societies. He was the organizer of the emigration movement, recruited the majority of Dutch emigrants, gave increasing momentum to what had perhaps begun as an idle thought; he was, in short, the publicizer, and he often did it for money.

Every Canadian immigrant had the potential to become an emigration agent. The letters he wrote home about the conditions in the new land had a tremendous impact on the circle of friends and family he left at home. If the reports were positive and optimistic others would inevitably react to them in a favourable way. The Dutch Canadians were no exception to this rule: they wrote home as soon as possible and often their letters appeared in hometown newspapers without any evaluation. As early as 1894 negative reports about inadequate pay for farm hands were published in Dutch newspapers. The Canadian Department of the Interior realized the detrimental effects of such material on recruitment, and, while trying to satisfy the most vociferous complainers, it also supplied interested individuals, societies, and newspapers in the Netherlands with more positive information about Canada.[14] But these efforts were continually counteracted by the bitter personal commentaries appearing in the Dutch press. Long hours, poor employers, the hardships of homesteading, loneliness, and the bitter weather of the Prairies took the gilt edge off the more optimistic reports and observations.[15] The majority of Dutch immigrants were positive about their experiences and although some remained guarded in their statements, the majority envisioned ultimate success. Such success, they noted, was no longer possible in the Netherlands. The Canadian government gave some thought to recruiting successful Dutch-Canadian farmers for public lecture tours in the Netherlands to counteract the negative publicity, but whether due to inadequate funds or the smallness of Dutch emigration they decided against it. Emigration recruitment was to be left to private enterprise.

Private enterprise thought that recruitment in the Netherlands was worth an extra effort. The Canadian Pacific Railway paid bonuses to all its representatives in Europe for each emigrant who travelled with the company. Dutch Canadians such as J. Holtrighter of Carlyle, Manitoba, received commissions on the ship and rail travel undertaken by those people he convinced to come to Canada on his visit to the "old country."[16] Other Dutch Canadians received a free trip in return for recruitment activities. If such agents combined bonuses, free trips, and the sale of land in Canada with fees from Canadian farmers for finding farm hands, trips to the Netherlands could and did become profitable ventures.

Booking agents representing transportation companies in the Netherlands also served as emigration agents. They supplied materials to interested parties about the services their companies offered, the countries serviced by their companies, and the opportunities available to immigrants. Companies such as the Red Star Line provided pamphlets and brochures about Canada while the CPR could offer steamship and rail transportation and even farms in Canada. As the Dutch had no regulations prohibiting or regulating such propaganda, the field was wide open to exaggeration, obfuscation, and lies. The transportation companies and their agents were interested in numbers and profits and showed little real concern for either the quality or the fate of their recruits.

Without exception, the most successful agents were those who could claim Canadian experience and were backed by a Canadian company. Such men, returning to their home districts, merited a certain respect. The fact that they were fellow countrymen who had made good in Canada added credence to their message. Their own hard work and perseverance had brought them financial rewards, a respected place in the Canadian society, and a chance to give that same opportunity to others. Simply because financial interests were involved in the recruitment did not mean that the philanthropic gesture was unappreciated. They were, after all, men who shared their culture, language (even dialect); they understood the longing for land and security; they would not cheat the prospective immigrants.

If the agent was able to combine certain aspects of religion with his recruitment he tended to be even more successful. Orthodox Protestants and Roman Catholics readily responded to those agents who were able to point to their concern for spiritual as well as economic necessities. The application of a holy gloss over economic longings made the decision to leave the Netherlands just that much more palatable, and, more importantly, it provided a continuity of life that promised to retain a certain measure of stability in the emigrant's disrupted life. Many agents used religion as one more tool in their battery of tricks to create the feeling of trust that was so necessary to their work.

To achieve trust was, of course, difficult, given the warnings in the public press and the more accurate information of the Netherlands Emigration League. Agents tried to avoid blatant lies and dealt in more defensible half-truths. The problem with their activities was not so much what they said but what they left unsaid. The most vivid example of the use of misleading information involves the settlement of Dutch Catholics on the so-called "irrigated farms" of the CPR at Strathmore, Alberta. In 1908 the CPR retained a Dutch priest, Father Van Aaken of Helena, Montana, to tour Catholic areas in the Netherlands to recruit immigrants. Van Aaken emphasized the possibility of owning good lands in a colony settlement where the Catholic faith could be preserved. Because of his priestly calling the response was great and he managed to recruit almost 100 families in two years. What Van Aaken failed to point out was that the land was, for the most part, unbroken and in a primitive state of irrigation, that the growing season was short, and that he had no intention of staying to help establish the colony. Due to inexperience, weather, and shortcomings of the CPR, many settlers failed to achieve any real success and some drifted away from the settlement and lost their stake while others stayed to tough it out. Van Aaken disappeared, no doubt with his commission in his pocket.[17]

Father Van Aaken was followed in 1910 by George Louis Boer, a former water inspector for the CPR at Strathmore. He was appointed colonization manager of the Land Colonization Branch in the Netherlands for the CPR and lectured in the Catholic areas of the Netherlands during the winter and spring of 1911 and 1912. His successful position and knowledge of the Strathmore area, combined with a facility for painting a glorious future on the Prairies of Canada, brought a heightened interest in Canadian settlement.[18]

Boer, like Van Aaken, made the homesteading process sound easier than it really was. He underestimated by half the capital needed for a good start in farming the "irrigated" farms. He said nothing about the problems that former settlers had had with the CPR. He underplayed the physical endurance and stamina required to farm 160 acres of unbroken land and intimated that even non-farmers could easily accustom themselves to the demands of the job. Perhaps worst of all, he urged his recruits to buy land immediately upon their arrival in Canada even though it was a generally accepted rule that Europeans should spend a year, at least, working on a Canadian farm to learn the very different dryland farming methods.[19] It is little wonder a Dutch-Canadian observer, Willem de Gelder, described the whole business as a "swindle."[20]

An agent's job had only just begun once he had recruited a sizable group of emigrants. He had to make sure they acquired all the necessary documents to leave Netherlands and he had to make travel arrangements on ship and on train to get them to their destination. He sold them railway tickets at a higher cost in the Netherlands than those that could be obtained at the Canadian dockside. Baggage and personal goods had to be routed to the correct destination and a thousand and one details needed to be checked out. Then, and only then, would he accompany his group of emigrants to Canada. He would act as interpreter, guide, facilitator at customs and immigration, and general factotum and would attempt to keep the group together and away from other agents and operators at the ports and stops. These "sharpers," some of whom were Dutch, offered work and land, but they were primarily interested in acquiring a part of the immigrant's bankroll. Most of them were freelance agents who depended on their own quick wits to sell poor land or offer jobs for which they received commissions from employers. This type of agent met every boat in the seaports and every train in the important cities across Canada. No doubt, when the group reached its destination, minus the few who had not survived the gauntlet of importuning, the primary agent heaved a sign of relief. He still had work to do in that he tried to sell land, and then sought to find farm work and accommodation for those who could not or would not buy, and he also had to see to the general settling in of his charges.[21]

A significant number of people saw some benefit in the recruitment of emigrants from the Netherlands. While the private emigration societies saw their own activities as philanthropic and altruistic, it is clear that much of their motivation was based on a desire to relieve the Netherlands, by emigration, of a potentially disruptive group of people. Emigration, more and more, became regarded as a social mechanism to retain a balance in society. Those who ran the organizations were not of the affected classes but assumed they knew what was best for the unemployed and disadvantaged. One can speculate that the failure of emigration to grow in the 1890-1918 period is due to the fact that many of those who were the object of the recruitment did not see emigration as a relevant or viable answer to their own peculiar needs.

NOTES

1. Detailed accounts of Dutch-American immigration can be found in H.A. Lucas, *Netherlanders in America* (1955), and the *Harvard Encyclopedia of American Ethnic Groups* (1980).
2. R. Insinger to L. Pereira, 18 February 1892, Department of the Interior (Immigration Branch) Records, Public Archives of Canada, Ottawa. These Immigration Records hereafter noted as DI/IBR, PAC.
3. B.H.M. Vlekke, *The Evolution of the Dutch Nation* (1945), p. 322; W. Van Horne to the Department of the Interior, 26 June 1894, DI/IBR, PAC.
4. R. Insinger to the Department of the Interior, 18 February 1892; H. Dixon to the Department of Interior, 15 July 1892, DI/IBR, PAC.
5. Department of Interior to R. Insinger, 25 February 1892, DI/IBR, PAC.
6. L.R. Nepvan to the Department of Interior, 2 June 1892, DI/IBR, PAC.
7. K. Boissevain to Clifford Sifton, 12 April 1897, DI/IBR, PAC.
8. "Annual Report of the Haarlem Emigration Commission, 1914," Netherlands Emigration Service Collection, Glenbow-Alberta Institute, Calgary. (This collection hereafter cited as NESC, GAI.)
9. Ernest Parr to the author, 12 September 1973.
10. J.C.C. Sandberg, "Emigration, A Burning European Question," *Economisch-Statitische Berichten*, NESC, GAI.
11. J.A.A. Hartland, *De Geschiedenis van de Nederlandse Emigratie Tot De Tweede Wereldoorlog* (1959), pp. 16, 26, 46.
12. "Emigration to Middle Canada," *Handelsberichten*, 563 (27 December 1917); J. Maurer, "Trip Report on Nova Scotia and Western Canada, 1915," NESC, GAI.
13. Hartland, *De Geschiedenis*, pp. 50-52.
14. *Ibid.*, p. 50; "Emigration to British Possessions," NESC, GAI.
15. K. Boissevain to Clifford Sifton, 12 April 1897, DI/IBR, PAC.
16. J.I. Ross to G. Turriff, 19 December 1904, DI/IBR, PAC.
17. Willem de Gelder, *A Dutch Homesteader on the Prairies* (1973), p. 41; J.B. Hedges, *Building the Canadian West* (1930), pp. 209-10; Hartland, *De Geschiedenis*, p. 51; Maurer, "Trip Report," p. 42.
18. G.L. Boer to the Central Emigration Foundation Holland, 8 March 1924, NESC, GAI.
19. Maurer, "Trip Report," pp. 38-41.
20. De Gelder, *A Dutch Homesteader*, p. 41.
21. *Ibid.*, p. 38; Vice-Consul Groenman, "A Report regarding the possibilities for Netherlanders in Canada, 1913"; G.L. Boer to the Central Emigration Foundation Holland, 8 March 1924, NESC, GAI.

TWO

The Early Settlers

CANADIAN IMMIGRATION POLICY

Prior to 1896, Canadian immigration regulations prohibited the entry of "the diseased, the criminal or vicious and those likely to become public charges." These rules were applied only to those who entered at seaports as steerage passengers, for there was no inspection of first-, second-, or third-class ship passengers or of those entering from the United States. Distinctions according to occupation were not made. While immigration policy was not restrictive, certain types of immigrants were clearly preferred. Agriculturalists who could settle and develop the Canadian Prairies were given the first priority.[1]

The Canadian government made it clear that it approved of the entry of the Dutch. Minister of the Interior Edgar Dewdney regarded "the people of Holland as a specially desirable class in the North West, being particularly adapted to the system of local self-government everywhere in vogue in this country."[2] This view of the Dutch clearly made them "white men" and not "foreigners" and therefore a people who would fit into Canadian society without any problem. The unstated assumption was that the Dutch were racially and culturally acceptable and shared the same values of respect for peace, order, and good government as Canadians. This attitude did much to ease not only the immigration of the Dutch but also their acceptance into Canadian society. It subtly expressed the belief that the Dutch by inheritance were members of the obviously superior Anglo-Saxon race. While they were not English they were "Nordic" and Saxons and their societies exemplified the pinnacle of evolutionary development at the turn of the century. The scientific, economic, political, and social advances of western European societies indicated not only the rise of the "fittest" to the top but also the arrival of the most superior societies ever to make their appearance on the stage of world history. Clearly, the Dutch were to benefit from such pseudoscientific racial stereotyping.

The accession to power in 1896 by the Liberal government of Wilfrid Laurier marked a further development of Canadian immigration policy.

17

Clifford Sifton, the new Minister of the Interior, was the architect of this policy. He believed the West was to be Canada's future source of national prosperity and that this potential would only be realized if the Prairies were settled by the right kind of people, that is, farmers and farm labourers. Sifton's policy was not so much a change from that of previous administrations as a vigorous restatement. Economic development had always been important but his preferences for agriculturalists made it clear that immigrants would be more carefully chosen to encourage the settlement of the West.

To this end Sifton began an active campaign to refurbish existing immigration regulations, build up the immigration department, and recruit agricultural immigrants. He had no desire to turn Canada into a refuge for the indigent urban worker or the professional, neither of whom had agricultural experience. He left no doubt as to his position: "It takes two generations to convert a town-bred population into an agricultural one. Canada has no time for that operation."[3]

Sifton regarded northern Europe as the most desirable source of immigration after the United States and Great Britain. However, by 1900, many northern European countries, such as Germany and France, restricted emigration. Since the Dutch government had no such prohibitions, it became an important field for Canadian recruitment. It soon became evident, however, that apart from farm labourers, no great numbers were prepared to emigrate, despite critical economic conditions at home.

Steamship company booking agents handled the recruitment of farmers and farm labourers in Holland. They also carried out a rudimentary screening process, based primarily on the applicant's occupation and health. As early as 1897 the Department of the Interior had considered appointing a Dutch Canadian as immigration representative to the Netherlands, but the traffic would not justify such a placement until the 1920's.[4] So the agents continued the recruitment. They were paid by the Canadian authorities a £1 commission for each bona fide farmer or domestic, most of which was remitted to their companies. The CPR also paid its agents in the Netherlands to recruit farmers and domestics.

THE FIRST ARRIVALS

The arrival at Saint John or Quebec after a ten- to fourteen-day journey was often a longed-for event. For some it was a welcome relief from nausea and illness, but for others it was the first opportunity to catch an exciting glimpse of the new homeland. The embarkation became a blur of events punctuated occasionally by lost baggage, the formalities of the immigration and customs inspection, and the necessity of finding the right train. Most immigrants spoke no English, and if they were without an interpreter or guide, the day became increasingly more hectic and confusing. At last, seated in a colonist car, with tickets of destination tied to their clothing, they were ready to proceed. Doubtless it was only then that they discovered that food was unavailable on the train and they would have to return to the platform for such essentials as bread, sausage, and jam. At every stop in the train's progress a mass of men descended upon the platform peddlers to buy food. Those who were accompanied by an English-speaking guide had a comparatively easy journey. But the very first immigrants were on their own.

The immensity of Canada was unnerving. Unlike the Netherlands, distances between cities were measured in days and not minutes. The farm land seemed sparsely settled among the endless acres of trees. Popular conceptions of Canada held by most Dutchmen seemed to be true. Distances were unimaginable, and it was not difficult to believe that this nation was inhabited by Indians and Eskimos with a sprinkling of white people. The pockets of civilization were swiftly swallowed up by the beautiful but threatening forests. It was hard to believe that agriculture could be a rewarding occupation in such a land.

Slowly but surely the train moved west toward Winnipeg. The city seemed as far away and unreachable as had the seaports a few short days before. The crowded wooden seats of the trains and the ever-present dust and smoke from the locomotive transformed the awaited city into an inviting oasis. Winnipeg was the "gateway to the West," a railway terminus in which most of the immigrants would have an opportunity to get a good night's sleep in the Immigration Hall and a chance to wash themselves and their clothes. From here they would be directed to their final destinations. Those without prearranged jobs would be helped by a resident employment agency to find suitable work. Those who were interested in homesteads were offered land and sent on their way. Those lucky enough to know someone in Winnipeg ended their journey there and settled down to begin their new lives. Winnipeg was the second port of call, but the most important one for the new immigrants.

In the spring of 1893, a group of single Friesian agriculturalists arrived in Winnipeg. They were the vanguard of a larger group of Dutch immigrants who had been aided by the Christian Emigration Society to go west to Yorkton, in the Saskatchewan area, to take up homesteads. To supplement their income, they took jobs on the railways and as hired farm hands and began the arduous process of accumulating settlement capital. Only a small number of this group actually went to the Yorkton area to establish homesteads or take up jobs. Most of them settled in and around Winnipeg, hoping to do as well or better in the more populous districts of Manitoba.[5]

For those who did go on to Yorkton, life was extremely difficult. They felt lonely and isolated not only on the Prairies but also in their jobs. Both language and work were unfamiliar, and they became increasingly dissatisfied with their new jobs and fearful for the future. Klaas De Jong, one of these immigrants, wrote home describing the fate of a companion, a railway worker who had written an optimistic dispatch to his hometown newspaper.

> The writer [is] already dead and buried on one of the highest hills in Medicine Hat. He lay in the hospital there and the foreman brought him

a pass and told him that in an hour he would have to be at the station to go back to work on the next train. He went downstairs to wash up and suddenly fell down, never to stand up again . . . so far from home and only twenty-seven years old.[6]

Even De Jong, who was used to hard work, found the challenge of working and homesteading to be too great. Unwilling to endure the work and certain that life in the Far West held no promise for him, he joined the other immigrants who were making their way back to Winnipeg.

In Winnipeg these immigrants were joined by single men and families who had found homesteading in Manitoba just as difficult. Nothing remained but to try for jobs in Winnipeg or to hire out as hands on local farms. As early as 1895, some saw an opportunity to make a living by peddling fresh vegetables in the city. Gathering capital together for a horse and cart proved difficult, but eventually the Dutch peddler made his appearance on the city streets. Successful in sales, the immigrants began to explore the possibility of growing their own vegetables and increasing their profits. Somehow more money was gathered to rent land, and by 1905 several Dutch Canadians were growing and selling vegetables and produce in the Winnipeg area.[7]

The vegetable-growing areas were centred in the Winnipeg suburbs of Elmwood and East Kildonan. While most of the land was rented, a few successful peddlers owned fifty or sixty acres farther out from the city and some employed other immigrants as farm labourers. But most growers ran a one-man operation; they owned a cart and horse, tools, and perhaps a greenhouse. They depended on their own or family labour to make ends meet and could look forward to some economic advancement. The short growing season forced the small producer to look for other work in the winter months either in the city or on neighbouring mixed farms. Above all, the fickle weather of the Prairies and the cold winters made this type of business a risky venture.

These immigrants formed the nucleus of a growing Dutch community in Winnipeg. Their correspondence with friends and relatives brought others to Canada to try their luck. Some even brought over their parents, much to the subsequent regret of the old people, who found the adjustment to Canadian life extremely difficult. But the Dutch community grew and so did the desire to help those immigrants who continued to regard Winnipeg as a haven from failure. An organization was set up to give aid to needy immigrants and provide social and cultural activities for the community. It established the Queen Wilhelmina Fund to give temporary financial aid to immigrants in distress.

Religion was also an important concern of the immigrants. Since there were no Dutch churches in Winnipeg in the early years, many Protestants attended Presbyterian or Methodist churches. Some became communicant members of the Canadian congregations, but others remained interested in establishing a Dutch church where sermons would be preached in the native language. Because of a lack of finances and members, renting a hall and supporting a minister was impossible. Services took place in private homes under the direction of church elders and were attended primarily by the Dutch Calvinists. Roman Catholic immigrants often attended local churches, but despite the Latin mass, language again prevented many from becoming active members.

By 1905 it seemed clear to some that they had to choose between assimilation into the Canadian churches and the loss of their traditional religious practices or the establishment of their own Dutch church. This choice was most obvious to the Calvinist immigrants. To preserve their faith, they organized the Winnipeg Christian Reformed Church in November of 1908. With the aid of the Iowa Classis (Presbytery) of the Christian Reformed Church of America, regular visits by American ministers were arranged. Meetings were held in rented rooms and halls. The visiting minister stayed for two or three weeks, preaching, serving communion, officiating at marriages and baptisms, and giving guidance and advice. During his absence, church elders were permitted to read published sermons. After three precarious years, Winnipeg was designated a missionary field by the Christian Reformed Church and a missionary pastor was posted there in 1911, with minimal financial aid from the congregation. A parsonage was purchased, and in 1912 the congregation built a church in Elmwood to serve the greater Winnipeg area.[8]

The Dutch church functioned as more than a mere religious institution. Through its deaconate, it gave limited but necessary financial support to its indigent members. Its clubs, youth groups, and choral organizations provided social activities for local immigrants. New arrivals found a responsive bit of their native culture alive in the Canadian West and joined the church or its organizations. But as they became more familiar with Canada, the immigrants' dependence on the church lessened and the help of church members in finding jobs or homes became less necessary. A great many immigrants severed their connections with the church as they became integrated into Canadian society.

Over time the Dutch community also split along class and economic lines. Most of the immigrants were of the labouring classes and had come to Canada with little capital. Their financial success had been, for the most part, indifferent. Few, however, desired to return to the Netherlands, for they had found in Canada an acceptance not based on wealth and class but on personality and ability. One observer wrote that many were imbued with an "American spirit of independence." This democratic and independent spirit brought them in conflict with other Dutch or Dutch-American immigrants who pretended to a higher social or religious status based on their economic success. This group saw its natural role in the leadership of the Dutch community and church. The labourers were reluctant to hand over the reins of community organizations to their social "betters" and a deep division threatened to tear the community apart. The more democratic immigrants withdrew their memberships from the Dutch cultural organization and ceased to support the Queen Wilhelmina Fund. They also made demands for representation and involvement in church affairs, and the resulting conflict apparently precipitated the early departure of the first Christian Reformed missionary. This conflict widened the distance between already dissimilar Dutch immigrants and encouraged many to give up their ethnic identification.

The decline in the flow of new immigrants and Canadian suspicions about foreigners after the outbreak of the war contributed to the decline of the Winnipeg Christian Reformed Church. For many of its original adherents, it now appeared safer to merge into Canadian society than to continue to go to a foreign-language church. The lack of a resident minister after 1913 furthered the disintegration of the congregation. As early as 1913 it was estimated that few of the 1,600 Dutch immigrants resident in Winnipeg belonged to the Dutch-language church. Most of the immigrants either attended a Canadian church or maintained only social contact with the Dutch congregation.[9]

The Canadian government's active campaign to recruit farm workers to homesteads in the West also affected the Dutch settlements in Iowa, Michigan, and Montana. By 1890, the American Dutch had spread from Michigan and Iowa all the way across the nation to the state of Washington and had become an established part of American society. Settlement possibilities, however, had been diminished with the disappearance of readily available cheap or free land, and some of the Dutch Americans consequently began to look across the border for new opportunities. Settlers from Iowa and Montana decided to take up homesteads in the Nobleford and Leavings area of the Alberta territory. Among them were immigrants who had originally come from Nijverdal in the province of Overijsel. They moved to Canada in the spring of 1904 and arranged to meet a group of settlers who would be coming to join them later from the Netherlands. By March of that year the arduous process of settling in had begun.[10]

The area was semi-arid but seemed to have good soil and sufficient rainfall for the cultivation of wheat, flax, and barley. There was also sufficient range to run cattle. The immigrants from the Netherlands were fortunate that the Dutch Americans had dryland farming experience. They were familiar with the requirements of homesteading and became an invaluable source of information and support, giving advice on land purchases, providing temporary accommodation to newcomers, and helping them purchase supplies, equipment, and horses. Most importantly, they provided encouragement and aid when the spirits of the settlers threatened to falter.

The settlement in the Nobleford area was christened Nieuw Nijverdal and was typical of much of the homesteading undertaken by groups, as distinct from the predominantly single settlers in Yorkton and Winnipeg. The immigrants settled on independent homesteads but depended on each other for help and advice. The first task to be tackled was the building of houses. The Dutch Americans were familiar with the methods and instructed their newly arrived countrymen. One such house-raising was described by the daughter of a newcomer:

> My Dad left one morning early and it was fifteen miles to our land. When he got there, he measured a piece of land 12 foot by 12 foot and put fence posts around it. I think there were eight of them but there may have been more. Then he nailed boards all around and after that the roof went on, without shingles of course. . . .[11]

At a later date a door and a window were cut in the walls and a hole in the roof for the stovepipe. The roof was shingled and the walls were insulated with ploughed-up prairie sods. This little shack housed two adults and five children for the first three years.

While the men began to break the required ten acres of land with their new horses and ploughs, the rest of the family was busy trying to organize the household. The children were sent to gather cowchips dropped by free-ranging cattle belonging to Canadian homesteaders or ranchers. Driftwood, gathered in the river bottoms, augmented the dried manure as fuel. The older children hauled water for drinking and washing from the river and sloughs. Cleanliness was not impossible in a dirt-floored shack but it was highly improbable, and housewives found it to be a constant struggle simply to maintain minimal standards. While the men had to learn new farming techniques, many women had to learn to bake bread. Most Dutch villages had had a resident baker who delivered in the surrounding countryside so that baking bread had never been a necessary skill even for farm women. The American housewives gave the newcomers simple instructions, but the initial results were often far from satisfactory. As time went on, the quality of the bread slowly improved.[12]

After the men finished breaking, discing, and seeding, they took jobs as farm hands with their more prosperous and settled neighbours. Any extra income was welcome, and some walked many miles to and from work and spent a long hard day in the fields for one dollar and meals. The extra income was critically necessary because most of the capital had been spent on the shack, horses, and equipment. Very little money remained for food, and during the first year many settlers subsisted on bread and pancakes with the occasional addition of a little sugar, milk, and oatmeal if work was plentiful. Wild game apparently was scarce and seldom graced the table. The seeding and harvesting seasons brought opportunities for well-paid work and the extra income helped the settlers eke out an existence during the winter months.[13]

Sickness was an ever-present danger; it could mean an unwanted dependence on neighbours or possibly a threat to the whole family's survival and an end to homesteading. Women found little release from their unending toil and the loneliness of the Prairies seemed to press down upon them. Going to town or visiting a Dutch-speaking neighbour was often difficult to arrange and letters from home only seemed to increase their homesickness. The letters all too vividly reminded the women of the neat farms and homes of the Dutch countryside and towns, which had sheltered friends and relatives.

Only the children seemed to make a rapid adjustment to their new life. As new land was settled, the homesteaders got together to establish local schools. The children found themselves learning English along with the children of other settlers who had come from Europe, the United States, and other parts of Canada. They quickly became proficient in the language and began to take on the values and ideas of their new society. The changes in their children dismayed some parents and magnified the loss of their native land and culture and made them question the wisdom of their move to Canada.[14]

The church, both in its religious and social functions, helped the immigrants to withstand many of the difficulties they had to face. Almost as soon as the Dutch settlers had arrived on their land, reading services were instituted in central locations and the small homes became crowded with neighbours and children. In 1905, a Christian Reformed minister arrived from Manhattan, Montana, on a visit to the Nobleford community. He preached, served communion, and baptized a number of children. The whole Dutch community was present, even those who were not members of the Christian Reformed Church. The services were as much social as religious events. When discussions were begun about the possibility of establishing a Christian Reformed church, the community split along the old religious divisions that had existed in the Netherlands. Some immigrants were in favour of holding religious services but objected to an affiliation with the Christian Reformed Church of America because they believed it was too conservative in doctrine. Nevertheless, a congregation was organized in Nieuw Nijverdal and it was intermittently served by ministers on classical appointments and seminary students on summer vacation. In the early years, services were held in homes and local schools and the costs were borne by the Board of Home Missions of the Christian Reformed Church and the Iowa Classis.[15]

The weekly church services were well attended, even though many families were forced to make a twelve- or fifteen-mile journey over prairie trails to attend. The church was the one local institution that brought most of the Dutch settlers together at least once a week. Its meetings, religious services, and organizations provided the companionship so necessary to the settlers, whose homesteads were often separated by miles of empty prairie or the intervening farms of non-Dutch settlers.[16]

From the very beginning, the Dutch community sought to attract other Dutch settlers to the homestead lands in the Nobleford area. Many immigrants wrote letters to friends and to newspapers in the United States and the Netherlands urging emigration. Homesteads and aid were offered to all who would come to help them in this venture. Church papers carried descriptions of the community and stressed the ongoing religious concerns of the homesteaders. Some settlers made visits home to the United States and recruited settlers from the Dutch communities in Montana, Iowa, Michigan, and Massachusetts. Letters to friends and relatives in the Netherlands also brought positive responses and the population in the community began to grow. Approximately two-thirds of the Dutch settlers attended the local Christian

Reformed services while the remainder were unaffiliated with any church. As the church community grew, so did the necessity to split it into separate congregations to serve the widespread Nobleford area. In 1911, the original Nieuw Nijverdal congregation was divided into three separate congregations to serve the Christian Reformed settlers in Monarch, Granum, and Burdett, Alberta.[17]

The settlement of more and more Dutch homesteaders fostered the old religious divisions that had been present in the Netherlands. In 1901, those settlers who had been members of the Netherlands Reformed Church in Holland, but who had attended the Christian Reformed Church in Nieuw Nijverdal, broke away to form a Reformed Church in Monarch. In 1912, they built their own church and the older and more liberal Reformed Church in America began a slow growth in Canada.

The community as a whole prospered and grew in the years before 1914. By 1911, there were 904 Dutch people living in the Medicine Hat census district, which included Nobleford and stretched from Monarch east to the Saskatchewan border. The Dutch settlers began to achieve the economic security and independence for which they had worked so hard. Crop returns in the Nobleford area were high and good prices for their products permitted expansion and investment. More land, implements, and horses were purchased and more ground was broken and seeded. The settlers abandoned their shacks to the chickens and built roomier, more comfortable wooden homes. Barns replaced dugout stables and the community took on a prosperous look. Homesickness lessened as the community grew and conditions improved. The Dutch slowly began to cut their ties with the Netherlands and accommodate themselves to Canadian society.

The Dutch immigrants felt satisfied with what they had accomplished. They had taken undeveloped land, brought it into production, and made themselves financially secure. They had achieved a worthwhile status in Canadian society and at the same time had preserved those Dutch traditions and institutions they valued and cherished. They had tested their abilities and their endurance and had proven their competence.

As the Dutch immigrants became more familiar with Canada and Canadian life, they began to value certain aspects of their lives in Canada. While they might complain about the rigours and the hardships, they appreciated the freedom, the lack of class restraints, and the economic possibilities this new land held for them. Some immigrants had achieved a measure of economic success that would have been impossible for them in the Netherlands. The gardeners of Elmwood and East Kildonan were not adverse to letting people know that life in Canada had its social and economic rewards. They believed that Canada had ample free land for those who wanted it, and an immigrant with the will to work could, without regard to his social class, find success in whatever area he chose. The success of the Nobleford settlers seemed to strengthen the gardeners' conviction. J. Maurer, the head of the Netherlands

Emigration League, was impressed by the Winnipeg residents' attitude and came to believe that the free and open society of Canada held as much, if not more, promise for suitable immigrants as all the free land.[18]

During the first two decades of the twentieth century, Dutch immigrants settled themselves in practically every province and major city in Canada. Their numbers were small in Nova Scotia, Quebec, and Ontario, although Montreal and Toronto each had a few hundred. But immigration into the area east of Winnipeg was negligible compared to the numbers who went to the Prairie provinces. The whole system of immigrant recruitment, whether governmental or private, was predicated on filling up and developing the western provinces. The "Golden West" was the "land of possibilities" and few immigrants saw much hope of economic advancement in the more developed eastern areas, which had fewer jobs to offer and no free or cheap land. Furthermore, Quebec and Ontario had only private employment agencies, which demanded a fee for job placement, while such services were free to those immigrants who applied at the employment offices of the Immigration Hall in Winnipeg. Those immigrants who had been recruited by CPR agents depended on the railway to place them either on land or in farm jobs. Quebec was often avoided by Catholic and Protestant immigrants alike. The former had been mistakenly warned by Church authorities in the Netherlands that French-Canadian Catholicism was the inheritor of the French liberal tradition and the latter seemed reluctant to settle in a Catholic and French province. The Maritimes, Ontario, and Quebec held little attraction for the farmers and farm labourers who wanted to get ahead.[19]

Except for Alberta, where there were 2,951 people of Dutch origin by 1911, the greatest number lived in Manitoba. Winnipeg was a beacon for those who wanted employment in an urban area, but many agriculturalists settled in the surrounding districts as well. Immigrants were to be found in Portage La Prairie, Morden, Argyle, and Rosebank and in other towns and settlements throughout the province. A group settlement was attempted in 1911 at Dog Lake, near Ashern, when seven Dutch families homesteaded the area. By 1915 they had organized a Christian Reformed congregation and the settlement had grown to 100 families.[20] Dutch and Dutch-American immigrants either took up homesteads in the province or worked as farm hands. Many were to move to the other provinces as new areas were opened up.

Both the Dutch and the Dutch Americans undertook to work and settle in Saskatchewan. In 1908, a group of Americans settled near Moose Jaw. They were followed in 1911 by a similar group that formed a community at Cramersburg, seventy miles north of Swift Current on the CPR line. As in Manitoba, the immigrants spread across the province. Observers have noted that there were Dutch immigrants in such places as Leoville, Swift Current, Morse, Cupar, Punichy, Saskatoon, Vonda, Regina. A number of families, direct from the province of North Holland, settled at Edam in the spring of 1914 and established a Christian Reformed congregation in 1917.

Alberta, as we have seen, attracted a significant number of immigrants after 1900. The beginnings in Nobleford in 1904 coincided with the movement of Dutch settlers to the Calgary and Edmonton areas. The settlement in Strathmore, under the tutelage of Father Van Aaken and George Louis Boer, began in 1908, and as in Manitoba and Saskatchewan, individual homesteading occurred all over the province. In the winter of 1912, a number of Dutch immigrants from Edmonton moved ninety miles northwest of the city to a tract of homestead land on which they founded the community of Neerlandia. By the summer of 1915, there were reputed to be a total of 700 Dutch immigrants in Calgary and Edmonton alone. It appears that the only settlement in British Columbia in 1915 was a group of fifteen families who had homesteaded in Golden with the help of the CPR.

Statistics and information about the majority of these settlers are simply non-existent. Travellers and visitors noted their presence in a particular area but have left no description of their work or their fate. The activities of such men as Van Aaken and Boer are poorly documented and the results of their recruitment are often described with bitterness because of the failure of the settlement. Little factual material has come to light about the experiences of the Dutch homesteaders, farm hands, or urban workers. Perhaps they were simply too busy making a living to bother recording the events of their lives or to speculate on their place in the development of the West. The immigrants have, for the most part, faded into anonymity.

Yet, two settlements, besides those in Winnipeg and Nobleford, exemplify the early Dutch experience in Canada: Neerlandia in Alberta, and the settlements in Nova Scotia founded in the second decade of the twentieth century. Settlers in both areas had the desire to succeed, yet the Nova Scotia settlements had disapppeared by the 1920's while Neerlandia was beginning to grow and prosper.

In the years prior to 1913, the Department of Agriculture of Nova Scotia became increasingly concerned with declining farm productivity and the accelerating abandonment of marginal agricultural areas. The department sent an agricultural representative, a Mr. Elderkin, to Ireland, Denmark, and Holland to examine the intensive methods of farming practised in those countries. Elderkin was also to study the co-operative systems used in the supply and marketing areas. On his return, he recommended that intensive farming and co-operatives be promoted in Nova Scotia and that immigrants be recruited in Europe to initiate such practices in Nova Scotia. The provincial government agreed to provide money for the recruitment and settlement of selected immigrant families. Elderkin returned to Europe and attempted to recruit experienced agriculturalists, but he quickly found that the Irishmen were not interested and that Denmark and Belgium prohibited immigration recruitment. Satisfied that the Dutch farmer had the necessary skills, he turned to the Netherlands.

In the Netherlands the settlement plan appealed to several Dutch families who had been considering emigration to Canada. Suitable farm families were to be individually settled on abandoned farms chosen for them by the Nova Scotia Department of Agriculture. Loans for household goods, living

27

expenses, seed, tools, and the mortgage on the land and house were to be extended by the government. The immigrants would begin to repay these loans from the proceeds of their first crop. The government hoped that the Dutch farmers would serve as an example to their Canadian neighbours, that they would prove that good crops could be produced by intensive cultivation and that marginal lands need not be abandoned.

The first five families arrived in the Annapolis Valley in the spring of 1914 and the Nova Scotia government fulfilled its promises. But it soon became clear that all was not well. The settlers had not been farm owners in the Netherlands but farm labourers. They displayed a penchant for buying equipment and furniture of the best quality without giving any consideration to the repayment of their debt. Furthermore, the farms on which they had been settled in Maitland and Selma were not of the promised quality but were often stony and overgrown. Much of the first year's work had to be given over to the reclamation and expansion of existing acreage, and thus the good harvests needed to pay off their debts were a practical impossibility. Transportation of their farm products to more settled areas for sale and processing was also difficult. The Hollanders in Maitland and Selma were forced to feed their apples to their pigs in the fall of 1914 because no sales organization existed to transport and sell apples even though the market price was high. The farmers in Selma had no outlet for their dairy products because the local creamery had previously been closed due to an inadequate supply of milk in the area. With the Department of Agriculture's help, the creamery was reopened before the year's end.

In the spring of 1915, five more Dutch families were recruited for farms in the Pugwash area. By this time the Nova Scotia government had learned its lesson. It specified that the immigrants be farm owners with a minimum of 4,000-5,000 guilders in investment capital. They were required to pay for their own household goods, living expenses, seed, and equipment and to provide 20 per cent of the farm purchase price. The Department of Agriculture hoped that by establishing these conditions it would get immigrants who would have a financial stake in their success and who would be less likely to spend their money unwisely. It was also becoming worried that it might see little return on its previous investments because $35,000 of the $300,000 budget had already been spent with little apparent result.

Like so many other settlement schemes in Canada, this plan was based on a hodgepodge of ideas and motives. The 1914 immigrants had seen it as an opportunity to acquire farms with the minimum of risk and investment. The support of the provincial government gave the project a legitimacy that other agents' plans did not possess. But they did not consider that their large debts made it almost impossible to succeed unless the crop yields and prices were at a maximum. It was soon apparent to everybody that mixed farming on marginal land would barely make ends meet. Those with large families of small children were in an even worse situation because their children were not old enough to hire out as domestics or farm labourers to supplement the family income. The ready availability of government money had led them into ruinous purchases and failure seemed a foregone conclusion.

The second group was composed of farmers, many of them with sons who also hoped to farm. They were encumbered with less debt and many felt that if they did not succeed, they could always sell out and go west. They understood the economics of farming, but were also disappointed by the quality of the land on which the government had settled them. They realized that the first years would be extremely difficult. But they remained hopeful and confident. Their problem was that they were too confident and arrogant. They refused to accept the advice of the local agricultural inspector on Canadian farming methods. Several settlers felt that Canadian practices were backward and inferior to the methods employed in the Netherlands. Their refusal to adapt cost many of them dearly.

The director of the Netherlands Emigration League, J. Maurer, visited the settlements in the summer of 1915 and was less than hopeful as to their fate. He believed the only advantage the Dutch in Nova Scotia possessed over western Canadian Dutch immigrants was that they lived in close proximity to each other. He predicted that the great debts would destroy the incentive to work and that the settlements would fail. His prediction was accurate. Even before the war ended many had abandoned their farms and moved to other parts of Canada. By 1920 all had left Nova Scotia, owing debts to the government ranging from $90 up to $6,000. Government overconfidence, immigrant conceit or inadequacy, and poor land and markets had destroyed the venture.[21]

Unlike the settlement in Nova Scotia, the founding of Neerlandia was undertaken by Dutch settlers who were familiar with Canadian life and conditions. The Dutch population of Edmonton had increased after the original settlement in 1904, and many immigrants found jobs in the city. But as the community grew, an increasing number of people began to dislike city life. Not only were most of the occupations menial, but the Canadian culture, they felt, was robbing them of their own language, culture, and religious distinctiveness. Many orthodox Calvinists regarded the church services as inadequate to stop the destruction of their religion. The secular public schools seemed to be filling their children with all kinds of heretical "liberal" thinking, the economic future looked bleak, and they missed the social closeness in an alien urban environment. Some who had previously attempted to homestead but had failed, and others direct from Holland, wanted to take up homesteads.[22]

In 1911, seventeen married and single men agreed to establish an exclusively Dutch colony north of Edmonton on good, fertile homestead land. They hoped that by keeping out other nationalities they would be able to run the local school in such a fashion as to preserve the finer qualities of the Dutch character. They planned to have a Christian Reformed church supported by all of the settlers. The preservation of the Dutch culture and the Reformed religion was to be accomplished by the co-operation of the homesteaders in all the facets of settlement. The men were to work together, and for each other, in a communal effort that would overcome the hardships of homesteading.[23]

When the men left to find suitable land in December, 1911, the women and children stayed in the Edmonton Immigration Hall and planned to join their men in the spring. Seventeen homesteads were staked out ten miles northeast of the railhead at Westlock, Alberta. The settlement was named Neerlandia in honour of their native land. Log houses and barns were erected using the heavy poplars and brush that covered the countryside. The men spent a year clearing and breaking the land and working as farm hands or labourers to accumulate the capital to continue the venture. The settlers traded work among themselves and established a church congregation. It was clear that co-operation, and the role religion played as a binding factor, kept the homesteaders going. A few settlers found the work too difficult and they were replaced by other settlers from Edmonton and southern Alberta. The economic recession of 1913 reduced available jobs in Edmonton and encouraged the unemployed to try their luck in Neerlandia.[24]

The influx of new homesteaders made possible the laying out of roads, the establishment of a post office and school, the building of a log church, and the formation of a co-operative society. The co-operative bought bulk supplies for the community and marketed cream, butter, and eggs to Edmonton buyers even though transportation of these products to market was difficult in the first years because of inadequate roads. Because wheat was especially difficult to transport, it was fed to cattle, which could be herded to the nearest railhead for transfer to the Edmonton stockyards. The community continued to attract settlers as the area was developed, and by January, 1916, sixty families were living in the Neerlandia area. The community was on a sound footing.

The financial success of the venture was matched by the gains made in the religious, educational, and social areas. Settlers supported the church and regularly attended the services, which were conducted either by elected elders or the visiting Home Missionary from Edmonton. The school was run by the local ratepayers, who appointed Willem Van Ark, one of the original seventeen settlers, as schoolmaster. Van Ark and the school board saw to it that the provincial curriculum was taught from a biblical standpoint. The activities of the church, the commitment to communal work, and the nearness of their fellow countrymen recreated a small part of the Netherlands in Canada for the immigrants.

A comparison of the Nova Scotia and Alberta settlements highlights some of the significant factors that determined the success or failure of all settlement in Canada in those early years. Clearly, it was best to start with as little debt as possible. This meant that the minimum in accommodations and equipment had to be accepted because most immigrants did not have a large starting capital. It was important to be as self-sufficient as possible in the first years so that any extra money might be reinvested in the farm. Perhaps even more important, some Neerlandia settlers had either Canadian or American farm experience. They were familiar with the type of land and with the methods and equipment necessary for a successful venture. The co-operative working, buying, and selling in Neerlandia contrasted sharply with the individual enterprises of the Nova Scotia settlers. The communal spirit in Neerlandia was strongly backed by the uniting influences of the church and school, and this proved to be a most significant factor in the colony's success. The Nova Scotia settlers, by contrast, had no real sense of community and no co-operation. The individual had to stand alone, exposed to the hazards of settlement without the benefit of church. Under such circumstances the economic and labour problems were magnified and personal adjustment to a new society was made more difficult. Those immigrants who chose to settle in communities such as Neerlandia and Nieuw Nijverdal had a much greater chance of achieving success than those who did not have the support of a common faith or the church.

THE SINGLE SETTLER

As the tempo of Dutch immigration increased in the twentieth century, many families made their way to the growing settlements in the Canadian West. An even greater number of single men came to take up labouring jobs in Canada. Some were interested in homesteading and realized the necessity of learning English, understanding Canadian farming methods, and accumulating the necessary capital to make a start. Others came simply for work and were content to drift from job to job and place to place without any real goal in mind beyond being self-supporting. Single homesteaders, farm hands, and labourers were to be found in practically every province in Canada.

Winnipeg was the great dispersal point for most of the Dutch immigrants. Men who had come with the Salvation Army were either sent on to farmers in the western provinces or were found jobs in the cities. The Salvation Army's employment bureau tried to match skills to available jobs, but often the placements proved to be a distinct failure. Most of the men did not speak English and were unfamiliar with Canadian work and customs, and thus they were at the mercy of their employers until they had acquired some work and language skills. Those who came on their own stayed in the Immigration Hall and went to the Dominion Lands Office to ask for jobs. The Lands Office had applications for farm labour and was able to tell the immigrants about their future employers and the work they would have to do. It appears that a job on a farm with other farm hands was preferable to being the only farm hand, as the latter circumstance often led to an excessive workload. Some men chose to work for the local Dutch gardeners or tried their luck in the city, but most decided to take the jobs that were offered to them at the Dominion Lands Office.[25]

For many farm hands life was incredibly hard. Long hours of physically trying work were aggravated by loneliness. Even good employers frequently made life difficult by their demands. When the harvest was over, only the best workers were kept on over the winter. In return for the odd jobs they might

31

do, they would receive room and board and perhaps a little tobacco money. Those without jobs had to go to the cities, to the mines and lumber camps, or to the railways for winter employment. Every fall Dutch farm hands drifted from place to place looking for jobs along with thousands of other farm hands. Some found employment and managed to eke out an existence. Others were unable to make ends meet and resorted to crime to keep body and soul together. That first winter also saw immigrants returning to Holland vowing never to return to Canada and promising retribution against those agents who had lured them on. The high hopes of spring had been replaced by cynicism and disappointment. The first year of work in Canada proved to be an effective winnowing process. The immigrants who withstood the hardships and remained in farming were better prepared for the following year. With a surer knowledge of farm practices and the language, they could demand higher wages and better conditions. Their increased earnings permitted the accumulation of capital and gave them the opportunity to homestead.[26]

As the single settlers became accustomed to their work and their neighbourhoods, they became, in many cases, active members of their communities. Without other Dutchmen around, they integrated quickly into Canadian society. Some men married local girls; others brought out brides or families from the old country. Attendance at local Canadian churches all but extinguished any cultural differences between the Dutch settlers and the Canadians. Those with orthodox Reformed religious leanings often found the process destructive to their faith and left their homesteads to congregate in the Dutch communities. More seemed content to surrender to the inevitable metamorphosis and accommodated themselves to their new homeland.

Single or married, drifter or settler, the early Dutch and Dutch-American immigrants had come to the "land of opportunity" for a second chance. They were the pioneers and the trail blazers for a movement that would grow in the following decades.

The First World War placed the Dutch community in Canada in somewhat of a quandary. Some immigrants held strong anti-English views as a result of the recent Anglo-Boer War. Some young men enlisted to defend their adopted country and served honourably on the Western Front.[27] Most, however, took a less active role, seeing their contribution to the war effort in the production of food and materiel. The Dutch Canadians do not seem to have stood out from their fellow citizens and most, it seems, benefited from the war with its high demands for goods and foodstuffs.[28]

NOTES

1. Joseph Kage, *With Faith and Thanksgiving* (1962), p. 62; Mabel F. Timlin, "Canada's Immigration Policy, 1896-1920," *Canadian Journal of Economics and Political Science*, 26 (November, 1960), p. 517.
2. The Department of the Interior to H. Dixon, 11 May 1894, DI/IBR, PAC.

3. John W. Dafoe, *Clifford Sifton in Relation to His Times* (1931), p. 323.
4. H. Dixon to Clifford Sifton, 12 April 1892, DI/IBR, PAC.
5. Lucas, *Netherlanders in America*, p. 460; DI/IBR, PAC.
6. K. De Jong to a friend, 1893, Martha Knapp Collection, Provincial Archives of Manitoba, Winnipeg.
7. Maurer, "Trip Report," p. 2.
8. Martha Knapp to author, 13 February 1973; A. Disselkoen, "A History of the Winnipeg Christian Reformed Church, 1890-1958" (1973), unpublished ms. in author's possession, pp. 1-2.
9. "Emigration of Hollanders to Canada," *Handelsberichten*, 11 (16 September 1915), NESC, GAI.
10. Maurer, "Trip Report," p. 11.
11. Mrs. John Hoffman, "Recollections," unpublished ms. in possession of the author. The bulk of the material pertaining to the Dutch settlement in the Nobleford area was provided by Rev. T. Hoffman of Grand Rapids, Michigan, during an interview in 1973; Lucas, *Netherlanders in America*, p. 461.
12. Hoffman, "Recollections," pp. 2-3.
13. *Ibid.*, p. 4.
14. Interview with Rev. T. Hoffman.
15. Hoffman, "Recollections," pp. 5-7.
16. Nobleford Christian Reformed Church, "The Golden Jubilee," pp. 1-2.
17. *Ibid.*, pp. 2-3.
18. Maurer, "Trip Report," pp. 12-15.
19. *Ibid.*, pp. 5-6.
20. Disselkoen, "A History," p. 2; Maurer, "Trip Report," p. 10.
21. *De Grondwet* (Holland, Michigan), 27 October 1908, 6 June, 11 July, 29 August 1911, 21 May 1912, Netherlands Museum Archives, Holland, Michigan; Maurer, "Trip Report," p. 10; *De Wachter* (Grand Rapids), 9 May 1917.
22. Maurer, "Trip Report," pp. 10-36; Hartland, *De Geschiendenis*, pp. 147-48.
23. Visit Report of W. Van Ark to the Netherlands Emigration League, 26 January 1916; J.J. Leys, *Nederlandsche Kolonisten in Canada* (1920); Anonymous, "Neerlandia" (no date), NESC, GAI.
24. W. Van Ark to J. Maurer, 17 February 1915, NESC, GAI; Memorandum from W. Van Ark to H.S. Kent, 11 January 1933; C.P.R. Colonization Files 1886-1940, Glenbow-Alberta Institute, Calgary.
25. Maurer, "Trip Report," p. 10; Vice-Consul Groenman, "A Report regarding the possibilities for Netherlanders in Canada, 1913," p. 38; De Gelder, *A Dutch Homesteader*, pp. 11, 38.
26. For a day-to-day description of a farm hand's life, see W. De Gelder, *A Dutch Homesteader on the Prairies*.
27. Interview with Mr. John Hoffman, Iron Springs, Alberta, 1978.
28. Interview with Rev. T. Hoffman.

PART TWO

The Wave, 1918–1939

THREE

Between the Wars: Why They Came

The First World War cut off practically all immigration from Europe, including the Netherlands, and the Canadian government took the opportunity to reorganize its immigration apparatus. In 1917 the Department of Immigration and Colonization was created as a separate department under the direction of James Calder. Undertaken in the expectation that immigration would reach new heights in the post-war period, the department was organized to meet the needs of the incoming immigrants more adequately. Immigration officials were to co-operate with officers responsible for the care and settlement of new immigrants. Dominion land officers were assigned to be in direct contact with arriving immigrants to facilitate the sale and settlement of government lands. A statistical branch was established in the new department to co-ordinate the collection of statistics from all the government departments dealing with immigrants. Hopefully, the past confusion about numbers and the inability to place any hard figures on entrants would now be done away with. By 1918 the department was ready for a renewed flow of immigrants.[1]

Canada was undergoing the unsettling transition from a war footing to peacetime life, but most Canadians remained confident that Canada would continue to grow and need suitable immigrants. As industries began to revamp for the civilian market, the wartime trends to urbanization and industrialization continued. The movement of farmers and labourers from the countryside to the city left a significant demand for thousands of agricultural workers and some skilled labourers. As a result, both the government and the transportation companies reactivated their European immigrant recruitment programs.

The pressures and constraints of the war years and the fear of a coming period of economic adjustment that might lead to unemployment and uncertainty were also forcing the Dutch to re-examine settlement opportunities in North America. Emigration to the United States in the post-war period appeared difficult. The demobilization of American troops and the subsequent moves to immigration restriction discouraged Dutch hopes in that direction. Rising nativism coupled with fears of Bolshevik revolution led to the passage of quotas in the United States Congress, which had the effect of restricting Dutch immigration to 3,602 persons by 1921 and to 1,646 in 1924. While the regulations were primarily aimed at slowing down the entry of southern and eastern Europeans, they effectively cut off the possibility of any significant number of Dutch citizens and redirected the interest toward Canada.

When those circumstances were combined with an active and unrelenting propaganda campaign, they produced the greatest immigration of Dutch citizens to Canada that had yet been experienced. From 1918 to 1930 over 15,000 Dutch citizens became new settlers in Canada. But the war, the lack of cheap land, and changing conditions in Canada made the immigrants hopes for economic betterment almost impossible. Most Dutch immigrants who came to Canada in this period did not substantially improve their economic condition beyond the position they had held at home. Economic stability and independence were often unimproved and emigration did not relieve the difficult conditions in the Netherlands. The decade that had seemed to promise so much for the immigrants in Canada after the bitter war years left most of the promises unfulfilled.

THE EMIGRANTS, 1918-1930

> Most of our emigrants are not reckless young people who throw themselves boldly into the adventures of a new and strange life. Naturally there are some among them, but most of them either quickly return or learn through privation and experience to accustom themselves to a set task. The great majority of Netherlands emigrants have outgrown the years of reckless and adventurous desire. They are mostly lower-middle class or labourers; store clerks who can look forward to no significant promotion; salesmen who have been put out of competition; small businessmen who are being pressed to death by larger companies; factory labourers who foresee a dreary life of hard work and no advancement whether for themselves or for their children; and especially farm labourers, who pulled by often enticing offers, supported by each others' example, often easily leave their district and homeland in large numbers.[2]

This passage, from a pamphlet written in 1913, captures the essential nature of the Dutch emigration movement as it developed before 1930. It was a movement based on the search for economic stability. The people who were most susceptible to economic fluctuation and change and had the fewest resources to contend with those forces were also those most interested in emigration propaganda. To them, Canada seemed a place of stable employment where one could rise above one's origins – a country of opportunity and free land, unrestrained by past tradition and practice.

Many young Dutchmen also regarded emigration as an escape from the perpetual drudgery of farm labour. The long hours and poor accommodation, even the poor food – meat once a week – could have been tolerated if the work had promised some future goal such as independence or eventual ownership of a farm. But for the Dutch farm workers, faced with intermittent unemployment, low wages and high costs, and an employer's frugal paternalism, even marriage seemed out of reach.[3]

For many young men it was not difficult to give up such a life. The opportuning of the transportation agent, the emigration society, or even Canadian government representatives, with their glowing descriptions of free or cheap land, thousands of jobs, and success dependent solely on personal initiative, seemed almost heaven sent. So the men took their most valuable possession, their labour, and left.

The same social and economic conditions that influenced young Dutchmen also had an effect on women. Occupational opportunities were limited in the city as well as in the countryside. The traditional role of women was limited to housewife and mother or to lower-status jobs as factory operatives. Advancement and training were practically non-existent for women, particularly if they competed with men for the same positions. Domestic service was poorly remunerated and marriage often was postponed by a simple lack of funds. Canada, however, offered well-paid employment for domestics in both urban and rural areas with the salaries running as high as $20 to $25 a month, wages comparable to those of an inexperienced farm hand. The demand was so great in Canada by the 1920's that eligible domestics were advanced 50 per cent of their passage money if they agreed to sign one-year contracts. The requirements were quite easy to fulfil. An applicant had to have sufficient money for travel costs, be between eighteen and thirty, and have a doctor's certificate of health and adequate experience, references, and a guaranteed job. Such jobs could be arranged in the Netherlands by the Canadian immigration office.[4]

Many young women saw a chance to advance themselves economically, see new places, meet new men, and have a little adventure. Others wanted to emigrate to join a fiancé or their family. Married women took up domestic service on arrival to supplement the husband's income during the critical settling period. While domestic servants most likely never made up more than 4 or 5 per cent of the total emigration from Holland to Canada, it was important to both the Canadians and the Dutch.

Emigration seemed to hold little appeal for the middle and upper classes; they tended to regard emigration as a desperate alternative suitable exclusively for those of the lower classes who could no longer contribute to Dutch society. It was precisely these middle- and upper-class people who became the leading proponents of emigration for other people, no doubt regarding it as a pragmatic and philanthropic answer to social problems.[5]

It is difficult to provide accurate documentation as to provincial origin of the emigrants. The greatest number seem to have come from the most heavily populated and industrialized province of the Netherlands, North Holland. This is the area where economic fluctuations affected both the urban industrial worker and the gardeners and farmers who supplied him with food. The struggle for land in the face of an ever-expanding industrial complex was also most critical here. The predominantly agricultural provinces of Friesland, North Brabant, and Groningen supplied the next largest group of emigrants. The smallest number came from the heavily Roman Catholic southern province of Limburg.

Regardless of provincial origin, social class, or occupation, the bulk of the emigration to Canada prior to 1940 was overwhelmingly single men or unaccompanied married men. Without family encumbrances, they would be willing to work as farm hands or on the homestead lands of the Prairies. The very nature of the work and the living quarters provided – shacks, bunkhouses, or farmers' attics – made the accommodation of a family extremely difficult. Wages were often not high enough to support a single farm hand, much less a family. Unlike in the more settled regions of the East, settlers in the West had not yet undergone the process of moving to better living conditions once the pioneer stage had passed. Even in the East abandoned log cabins and converted horse barns or chicken coops often had to serve as homes for those families who were brave enough to come in the 1920's. This separation of families and the lack of women would create problems in the coming years.

Among the single men coming to Canada were those who made up the "swallow emigration." These were primarily men from the province of Zeeland who made annual trips to southwestern Ontario in the 1920's for seasonal labour in the beet or tobacco fields. Such excursions were continued until enough money had been saved to buy or rent land in Ontario for permanent settlement.[6]

The educational level of most emigrants was not very high. The average emigrant had most likely completed elementary school, perhaps supplemented with apprenticeships, on-the-job training, or night courses. It is difficult to judge what the Canadian equivalent might have been, although some have argued it was certainly on the level of Canadian high school matriculation. If one uses the emigrants' letters circulated in the Dutch press as a yardstick, one can only conclude that the standard of literacy was high. In any case, the emigrants seemed to have enough formal education, native intelligence, and experience to meet their needs. Dutch emigration in this period, however, cannot be characterized as a flight of the highly skilled or educated.

Although the chief motivating factor for emigration was the desire for economic advancement, other considerations sometimes provided the spur. There were those who decided to leave simply because they "always had a longing to see far away places and lands, and [a desire to] live some of the adventures such as we read in books by James Oliver Curwood [and] Zane Grey."[7] Such adventurers tended to be less successful and determined than their more pragmatic compatriots and often ended up drifting after some ephemeral will-o'-the-wisp from city to city and country to country; but some did manage to settle down and face the realities of Canadian life. Probably even the most sober of emigrants looked forward to some adventure, some change and difference from their present life, something that gave an added fillip to what appeared to be a dangerous necessity.

Besides the more acceptable motives of emigration for material gain or adventure were less common ones founded in human desperation. Parents who thought their children's futures were jeopardized because of laziness, unsuitable companions, or involvement in petty crime sometimes delivered them into the not-so-tender hands of transportation agents for placement on farms in Canada. They must have believed that a period of time spent trying to survive on the prairie would teach the delinquent youth the values of hard work and the luxury of home. The black sheep sons of well-to-do families were occasionally given passage money to Canada and an annual remittance and told not to come home again. As is usually the case in such circumstances, the failure rate was high; Canada was no nursery or private boarding school for the rehabilitation of wayward youth.[8]

INDUCEMENTS TO EMIGRATE

The recruitment system for these prospective emigrants operated primarily in the Netherlands, but some propagandizing did come directly from Canada. The simplest type of recruitment consisted of newspaper advertisements in the Dutch press offering jobs or land and free information about Canada. The ads were placed by Dutch-Canadian farmers, farm labourers, or urban workers who received remuneration from transportation companies and farmers for each client they attracted. Little expense was entailed in this type of recruitment beyond advertising costs, postage, and paper.[9]

Organizations such as the Roman Catholic Holland Settlement Board and the Holland Colonization Board also advertised in the Dutch press. Others actively sought the endorsement of the Dutch religious emigration societies. Canadians such as Father K.E. Morrow of the Catholic Settlement League of Brechin, Ontario, claimed to have a mandate to settle Dutch Catholics on specified plots of land in Canada and just happened to be intimately connected to the Cunard and White Star lines. Father R.H. Dignan of Chatham was recruiter for a settlement in the Chatham, Ontario, area and representative of the CPR.[10]

The most successful recruiters were, however, agents of transportation companies or their representatives, and independent real estate agents in the Netherlands. Representatives of the White and Red Star lines, the Cunard Line, the Holland-America Line, and the Canadian Pacific all worked freely in the Netherlands. Most were simply interested in sending as many live bodies as possible on their respective lines. The CPR agent had the added incentive of a commission on transcontinental rail passage and the sale of land in Canada. He was, without a doubt, the most aggressive of all the recruiters and had the worst reputation.[11]

The independent real estate agents were interested in selling land to potential settlers. Usually they worked on commission for Canadian land or mortgage companies, although a few speculated with their own land. They received commissions on the land and on the ship and train transportation, and generally they were given free transportation and travel to and from the Netherlands. For many it was a paid vacation with great potential benefits.[12]

One of the great drawing cards of immigration prior to the depression was the claim that untold numbers of well-paid jobs were available in Canada. By the 1920's the lure of the homestead had diminished as the Dutch realized not only the difficulties of settling in but the reality that most of the good land close to the railways was gone. Many farm labourers and farmers came to believe that a job was the stepping stone to acquiring a sufficient stake to buy an operating farm. Agents and transportation companies realized that jobs rather than land were the best lure and that volume rather than quality was the necessary end of recruitment. It was easy enough to recruit non-agriculturalists and have them claim farm experience and a desire to farm in Canada.

As a result, agents recruited not only agriculturalists but also hairdressers, clerks, factory workers, barbers, cigar-makers – people who had rarely seen a cow, much less milked one. They told the recruits that the farm was only a stopping-off place to a better job more suited to the immigrant's work experience. They claimed that a few months work on the farm would give the immigrant a stake and a working knowledge of English, enabling him to go to the city and re-enter his former profession. Those who wanted to go to the United States, but who were prevented from doing so by the quota restrictions, were told that illegal entry was not at all difficult or impossible, although of course they would not counsel such action. The promises and information were as misleading as the immigrant's occupational declaration.[13]

The Netherlands was overrun by land sharks and immigration agents and bureaus that preyed on the Dutch public, seemingly without hindrance. Even the most experienced farmers and farm labourers fell victim to the blandishments of apparently upright and honest recruiters. Cornelius Cox, a failed Dutch-Canadian fuel dealer from Winnipeg, and his brother William, a Catholic priest, made repeated forays into the province of North Brabant to sell land and recruit immigrants for a Catholic parish in Manitoba. With a letter of introduction from the unsuspecting Archbishop of Winnipeg, they recruited settlers for Inwood and Plumas, Manitoba, in 1924 and 1927 and succeeded in bringing over a hundred people and tens of thousands of dollars to a marginal settlement north of Winnipeg. Having received their commissions from the Red Star Line and the Great-West Life Assurance Company, they abandoned the immigrants to their fate. Little wonder that the Roman Catholic Emigration Society regarded Cornelius Cox as "a double-distilled bandit." The helpless immigrants no doubt felt that his brother's actions bore a close resemblance to those of Judas Iscariot.[14]

Once the decision had been made to emigrate more mundane but certainly critical problems had to be surmounted. Some sort of financing had to be found to pay for the journey. Some municipalities regarded emigration as a way to relieve their welfare burden and manifested a rather indelicate haste to help the emigrant on his way. After 1923, with the establishment of the Central Emigration Foundation Holland (CEFH), the Dutch government in conjunction with some municipalities provided travel funds in return for a long-term loan agreement. Somehow or other money was scraped together and arrangements were made for the passage.[15]

The CEFH also made an attempt through its Canadian contacts to provide suitable jobs for agricultural emigrants. It was joined in this effort by the Land Settlement Branch of the Canadian Department of Immigration and the colonization departments of the Canadian Pacific and Canadian National railways. Independent agents, sometimes with the backing of Dutch municipalities, also attempted to find jobs for the prospective emigrants. All of them depended on Canadian provincial employment agencies where they existed. Practically no emigrant left Holland without some arrangement having been made for his employment in Canada. Needless to say, the arrangements were often as insubstantial as the glowing descriptions with which the agents had lured the emigrant.

With job and money secured, the most difficult duty remained, saying good-bye. Friends and relatives were visited, warnings of dire consequences suffered through, immeasurable amounts of gratuitous advice were tolerated, and the decision to leave was severely tested again and again. It was heart-wrenching to say farewell to parents and loved ones without the assurance that they would be seen again. Partings with fiancées or even wives and children were filled with displays of grief and promises of quick reunion. In most cases they had no real idea of what awaited them. Despite reputable information and warnings, even the most prepared emigrant was in for a culture shock. For many, emigration was a totally irrational step, a step that would lead them to a position from which there was no retreat. They would have to sink or swim by their own efforts and ability. Remarkably, most survived.

FIRST ENCOUNTERS

Practically all sectors of Canadian society regarded the Dutch as suitable settlers. Government opinion, as we have seen, favoured the Hollanders, and, as a Dutch emigration recruiter noted, "we know by experience that the Canadian government is anxious to have emigrants of the Nordic race, and objects to Russians and emigrants from Eastern Europe."[16] The Dutch seemed to be hard-working, law-abiding, rarely a charge upon public social services, and certainly never a disruptive element in Canadian society. Clearly, a Dutchman did not give cause for the rise of nativist fears about the inundation by inferior races. He was, in fact, considered practically equal to the average Canadian.

To even the most discriminating Canadian, it was evident that the Dutch practised modern hygiene standards. They were "clean," and as such welcome in every home, whether at the dinner table or in personal contact. They ate the same kind of food, practised the same rules of etiquette, and had few,

41

if any, disturbing personal habits. The Dutch appeared to be compatible and "assimilable."

Yet Canadians did have some questions as to the value of the Dutch immigrants. Labour unions, socialists, and Communists regarded non-agriculturalists as competitors in times of economic distress. While not all that many left rural employment after their arrival in Canada, their appearance in the cities was discouraged by unions and by municipal, provincial, and federal governments alike. The immigrants' willingness to take on any job created some friction, although the Dutch were seldom specifically singled out as a problem.

In his supposed area of competence, agriculture, the Dutch immigrant was regarded as a good worker and an outstanding colonist, even if he was sometimes an unnerving nuisance. The nuisance problem related directly to the sense of superiority many of the Dutch seemed to display toward Canadians and Canadian habits and practices. Not only did they feel Canada possessed no culture and few of the social amenities of life, but they had the gall to talk openly to Canadians about these things. Some immigrants felt they carried with them advanced techniques and practices that would bring tremendous benefits to Canadian agriculture. Naturally, Canadian farmers had little time or desire to listen to what they regarded to be the half-baked theories of newly arrived farm hands. True, the Netherlands might be more advanced in the establishment of co-operatives or in intensive farming, but these might not necessarily be relevant to the Canadian experience. Furthermore, on a personal level many immigrants felt innately superior to employers and this often led to unpleasant confrontations. Warnings by the Dutch emigration societies against egotism and self-conceit often fell on deaf ears. The societies realized that an immigrant's initial success or failure often set the tone for his following experiences. This culture conflict was usually a first-year phenomenon, for if the immigrant survived that year, he usually became aware of his own limitations and the need to adopt and value Canadian practices and attitudes.[17]

While the immigrant might point out the shortcomings of Canadian society, he generally regarded Canada as a Christian nation, one in which the dictates of conscience and religious belief could be met as they had been at home. Many quickly became active supporters of local Canadian churches and were welcomed by their fellow parishioners. Others, like the Orthodox Calvinists, while appreciating the interest of the Canadian churches, often chose to settle in areas where their co-religionists were already established. They felt it was difficult to maintain traditional doctrinal standards in the Canadian churches, whereas their Calvinist churches carried out no strange or disconcerting ritual or doctrine and gave no occasion for conflict with the mainstream of Canadian religious thought.[18]

The Dutch Protestant immigrants had a distinct advantage over their Roman Catholic brethren. Their belief, based as it was on a direct personal relationship with God, was not totally dependent on the services of a church or a minister, although such things enhanced and strengthened the faith. The Roman Catholics, however, in order to fulfil their religious obligations, had need of a Dutch-speaking priest. Until the immigrants learned to speak sufficient English to take their confession to a Canadian priest, they were unable to take communion and receive absolution.

Although some Dutch priests were to become emigrant recruiters, none were specifically assigned such duties or given active aid by the Canadian or Dutch church leaders. The Dutch Roman Catholic episcopacy generally oppposed emigration to Canada except under conditions in which religious obligations could be fulfilled. This view was to remain a distinct deterrent to Roman Catholic emigration until after the Second World War. It in no small measure accounts for the fact that Dutch emigration to Canada from 1890 to 1940 was predominantly Protestant in nature.[19] The less orthodox of both faiths worried very little about the disruption of their religious lives and the non-religious, no doubt, gave it no consideration at all.

The immigrants' attitude to education was generally acceptable to the host society. They seemed to place a reasonable value on learning, with emphasis on reading, writing, and arithmetic. The basically Christian outlook that was so important to the orthodox immigrant was not antithetical to Canadian thinking, as private and parochial schools were also available in a public-school–dominated environment. Immigrants found, to their delight, that local ratepayers controlled the local school boards and that, given adequate concentration of immigrants, policies could be established and teachers hired that would meet their particular needs.[20]

Most of all, Canadians were pleased by the immigrants' willingness to integrate. The Dutch laid stress on learning English and their children rapidly became Canadian in manner, attitude, and language. The Gerrits and Feikes quickly became Georges and Freds, and in some cases even last names were Anglicized, with Smit becoming Smith and Nieuwenhuis, Newhouse. Intermarriage, although acceptable to the Canadians, appeared to be met with some reluctance among the Dutch Orthodox Calvinists. But even here, reluctance often gave way to grudging assent on the part of the elders if the outsider became part of the Dutch church. The Roman Catholics, belonging as they did to a universal church and being more widely scattered, had few objections to a marriage outside the ethnic group as long as it was within the faith. Those with no church affiliation naturally saw no religious problem in intermarriage but shared with the rest an aversion to those other than western Europeans, whom they did not regard as equally blessed in matters of social and intellectual development.

The Dutch emigrants were somehow different from the other members of Dutch society. They shared with others the problems and disabilities of their society but, unlike the majority, they sought to escape. Perhaps they were, as some have suggested, the most energetic of their society; perhaps they were misfits.[21] In any case, they took with them a culture and a tradition essentially equal and acceptable to the Canadian society, yet it was a culture that inherently contained the seeds of conflict and division. The new life in the new land was to diminish the past and reorder the immigrants' existence, often in unwanted and irrevocable ways.

NOTES

1. Hedges, *Building the Canadian West*, p. 353; Norman Macdonald, *Canada: Immigration and Colonization 1841-1903* (1966), pp. 145-46.
2. A.L. Veenstra, *Emigratie en de Nederlandsche Vereniging Landverhuizing* (1914), p. 1, NESC, GAI.
3. K. Westra, "Life of an Immigrant," unpublished ms. in possession of the author, p. 1.
4. G.L. Boer to the Central Emigration Foundation Holland, 5 February 1924, NESC, GAI.
5. The Netherlands Emigration League to F.G. De Veer, 26 June 1925, NESC, GAI.
6. Hartland, *De Geschiedenis*, p. 147; T.H. De Meester, "Report on Dutch Immigrants to Canada, 1923-24," NESC, GAI.
7. J.W.A. De Boer, "This Land is our Land, It is the Land We Chose for Our Family," unpublished ms. in possession of the author, p. 4.
8. "Annual Report of the Netherlands Emigration League, 1916"; F.G. De Veer to the Netherlands Emigration League, 11 June 1924, NESC, GAI; De Gelder, *A Dutch Homesteader*, p. xii.
9. *De Maasbode*, 28 June 1929, NESC, GAI.
10. T.H. De Meester to the Netherlands Emigration League, 17 February 1926; *De Tijd*, 14 June 1929; *De Residentiebode*, 29 January 1929, NESC, GAI.
11. Morzer-Bruyns to R.N.C.A., 23 January 1926, NESC, GAI.
12. Maurer, "Trip Report, " p. 10.
13. Monteyn, "Report on Conditions," pp. 3-4; for some descriptions of individual cases, see Consul-General Schuurman to the Ministry of External Affairs, 16 August 1927, NESC, GAI.
14. For the complete story on the Cox brothers, see *Beunhazen* file in NESC, GAI.
15. Veenstra, *Emigratie*, pp. 4-5; Hartland, *De Geschiedenis*, p. 62.
16. F.G. De Veer to the Central Emigration Foundation Holland, 1 February 1926, NESC, GAI.
17. "Annual Report of the Central Emigration Foundation Holland 1925," NESC, GAI.
18. De Gelder, *A Dutch Homesteader*, p. xiii; interviews with Rev. T. Hoffman and Mrs. G. Kamp, Grand Rapids, Michigan, March, 1973; *Friesch Dagblad* (Leeuwaarden), 12 December 1928, NESC, GAI.
19. Central Emigration Foundation Holland to W.B. Roadhouse, 7 December 1927, NESC, GAI.
20. T. Cnossen to *Patrimonium*, 20 August 1925, NESC, GAI.
21. Interview with T. Cnossen by author, January, 1970.

FOUR

Settling In

THE IMMIGRANTS, 1918-1930

Slowly but surely interest in emigration began to grow after 1918, and in 1923 over 1,000 people left the Netherlands for Canada. As the Canadian economy improved, this number rose in response to ever brightening possibilities. Such possibilities, however, were not to be found in every part of Canada.

Despite Canada's desire to fill up the West with suitable farm workers, immigrants expressed less interest in that area than they had in the pre-war period. Not only was good land scarce but it was felt that "the homesteader's battle to survive is long and demands perseverance."[1] Many immigrants were not prepared to make the kind of personal sacrifice in toil, loneliness, and financial insecurity that a homestead demanded of them. Casting about for other areas where advancement might be less difficult, they turned to the East.

Settlement in the Maritimes, however, held even less appeal than the Prairies. Although more heavily settled and with a more temperate climate, the Maritimes had not been a successful place for previous Dutch settlers. Poor farm land, lack of markets, and industrial backwardness combined with the absence of any significant urban centres to create a stagnant economy. The most important deterrent was the lack of agricultural jobs. Needing immediate employment because of a lack of cash reserves, immigrants were compelled to look elsewhere during the most important immigration months of March, April, and May. For example, in 1925 Nova Scotia advertised a mere fourteen openings in March, compared to 1,026 in Ontario. Few immigrants were willing to live on their meagre stakes until the job situation improved and so they passed the Maritime provinces by.[2]

The number of agricultural jobs available in Quebec was only slightly better than in the Maritimes and those immigrants who chose to settle there generally chose the Montreal area. Since most of the Dutch immigrants were Protestant they had more in common with the English community than the

French and isolation from the mainstream French Catholic society was the logical outcome. The lack of opportunities in the agricultural sector and the dearth of cheap land merely confirmed most immigrants' negative opinion of Quebec.[3]

Given prevailing attitudes and the chance for ready employment in the agricultural area, it is little wonder that the immigrants turned to Ontario as the best possibility. Ontario's heavily industrialized society, based on a secure agricultural foundation, provided a wide variety of opportunities. Urbanization during the war had drawn many farm workers to the cities and had opened up the agricultural job market. Besides, the mixed farming practices of Ontario were familiar to Dutch farmers and farm labourers. The longer growing season and diversified production were conducive to yearly contracts, and these voided the need for finding alternative winter employment in the bush or on the railways.[4]

Ontario had further advantages in that farms were small, settlement concentration could be heavier, and the possibility of community life and even church formation was much greater. While the majority of immigrants were single men, families were also part of the movement and Ontario, with its better housing, was more attractive to married men than the Prairies. It is understandable, therefore, that Ontario became the focus of Dutch settlement in the 1920's.

When the Dutch arrived in Ontario their first need was to find jobs. Some came with letters of introduction from Dutch booking agents or transportation company representatives. Others had positions arranged through the Canadian immigration inspector in the Netherlands. Those without guaranteed jobs were forced to look for themselves, often going to employment agencies or to the Colonization and Immigration Branch of the Ontario Department of Agriculture. As often as not, the branch's agents sent the immigrants to a locally prominent Dutchman or the representative of the Central Emigration Foundation. While the Central did provide generally satisfactory placements to the immigrants, as much could not be said for the other agencies.[5]

It soon became apparent to many that the golden promises were figments of the agent's imagination. What often awaited them was low pay and poor living conditions. One unsuccessful CPR immigrant wrote that he "would rather be in jail [in the Netherlands] for six months, than have to work in Canada."[6] Even recruits of the Calvinist Emigration Society who had been placed in Canada by the Holland Reformed Immigrant Aid Society sometimes wondered which goal the society gave priority to, the personal financial security of the immigrant or the building of church congregations in Canada. It seemed to some that placements by this group were done more with an eye on the hereafter than on the present.[7] Most had no choice and buckled down to work while keeping their eyes open for alternative jobs; others surrendered to their anger, loneliness, or disgust and sought repatriation. The consul general of the Netherlands in Montreal could do little but fulminate against the activities of the agents and the poor placements and try to find a way home for the failures.[8]

The farmers of Ontario were no more altruistic when it came to hiring farm hands than the western farmers had been before the war. A letter received by the Dutch consul in Toronto in 1927 is typical of the requests made by Ontario farmers: "Can you procure for us a Hollander . . . , life experienced in dairy farming, age 30, single man, about average intelligence, lean with work and a fast mover, fast dry-handed milker, used to milking machines."[9] While this particular farmer offered good wages and conditions, others saw the immigrant as someone to be exploited. A farm hand in Chatham, Ontario, described his work in the beet fields as "slavery" and complained that he had to work twelve hours a day, seven days a week. He claimed that some immigrant families had turned to bootlegging and prostitution because they were unable to endure the work and could find no employment. Dutch newspapers also carried accounts from others who had been bilked and cheated by their employers. Apparently farming on shares was a dangerous practice, for some farmers had the crop seized for repayment of debts when prices were low. They would then buy the crop back at the bailiff's sale for one-third the going price.[10]

Most immigrants were more fortunate. They worked hard, managed to learn Canadian farming methods, and accumulated some experience and a little capital. A few managed to buy farms but most continued to be hired hands because the high cost of improved farm land in Ontario made purchase difficult. The farms of southern and southwestern Ontario, where Dutch settlement was concentrated, were often beyond the reach of even those who had brought capital with them. Some, who made the mistake of purchasing land immediately upon their arrival, fell victim to their own haste. Without Canadian farming experience, they often lost their money in the purchase of poor or marginal land or in farms too small to sustain them and their families or to offer a chance for advancement.[11] Faced with destitution and unable to foresee any possibility of success, they either tried their luck in the cities, sought to return to Holland, or looked to the West for a second chance.

The church did much to sustain the Dutch immigrants in Ontario, particularly the Protestants. While there were some Catholic immigrants, most were quickly absorbed in local parishes. This was especially true in the sugar beet areas of southwestern Ontario where there was an existing settlement of Flemish-speaking Catholics. The Protestants were dispersed on the vegetable, fruit, and dairy farms in the Hamilton district or the beet farms of southwestern Ontario near Chatham and London or near Essex or Sarnia. It was more difficult for them to keep any social contacts, and loneliness and alienation were pressing problems. In response to these needs, the Christian Reformed Church quickly established congregations in Hamilton (1925), Chatham (1926), Sarnia (1926), and Essex (1928). While these churches were generally too poor to support a permanent resident minister, they were served by missionaries, seminary students, visiting ministers, and elders. Somehow they managed to meet both the social and religious needs of the Dutch Protestant community. The majority of the immigrants responded with enthusiasm and often travelled great distances to attend weekly services. Meetings were held in convenient halls, churches, or private homes. Courtships were begun, marriages and baptisms solemnized, and discussions initiated about new jobs and opportunities. The support and involvement of non-church immigrants were welcomed and some community strength and solidarity were established. It was the one institution that reached out to these strangers in their own language and made this alien land a little more like home. Difficulties with employers, hard toil, and personal fears were somewhat assuaged and most immigrants returned home Sunday night spiritually refreshed.[12]

While the majority of immigrants in the 1920's chose Ontario as their destination, some continued to be attracted to the Prairies. Their first stop, in Winnipeg, brought them into contact with the oldest Dutch community in Canada; there, some decided to end their long journeys, and by 1929 the community numbered almost 5,000 people. Since housing was more readily available in Winnipeg, many immigrant families and single men stayed and found work in the city. The Department of Immigration regularly sent agricultural workers to the Dutch vegetable gardeners. The social advantages of an established Dutch community were important in determining whether an immigrant stayed in Winnipeg or went farther west. Many new arrivals preferred the security of Winnipeg to the uncertainty of life on the open prairies.[13]

Those immigrants who did decide to go further west could depend on a number of organizations to help them find work or land. The colonization departments of the railways and the representatives of the Department of Immigration and the Central Emigration Foundation, along with government employment bureaus, helped to locate jobs and land. With the establishment of the Holland Reformed Immigrant Aid Society in 1927, a broad range of services was available. These various agencies and representatives sent most of the immigrants to jobs and land in Saskatchewan and Alberta.[14]

Conditions in the dryland areas of these provinces, however, were not always conducive to further settlement. The early Dutch settlers, like many of their Canadian neighbours, had not completely mastered the techniques of farming in the semi-arid areas of southern Alberta. Yearly cropping had exhausted moisture in the soil. Strip farming, introduced by one of the early Dutch-American homesteaders, was often ignored in favour of large crops. A three-year dry spell beginning in 1917 had further diminished soil moisture, reduced crop yields, and permitted the ever-present wind to begin blowing away the soil. Crop problems were exacerbated by difficulties in transportation and sale of wheat and by a rapid decline in the Canadian economy. The dissolution of the Wheat Board in 1920 spelled an end to government-regulated sales of wheat and the economic slump, which began in 1920, lowered the price of crops and often made the profit margin simply too small to continue farming. Many Dutch-Canadian farmers decided to move on.[15]

Several Dutch families from the dryland areas of Alberta were resettled in newly developed areas around Monarch, Crossfield, and Bottrel, Alberta. Others chose to leave the Prairies altogether and moved to Abbotsford in British Columbia. As well, the Dutch-American settlements in the state of Washington, begun in the 1890's, had plenty of cheap land, sufficient rainfall, and Dutch churches. Homesteaders, unemployed farm hands, and adventurers left the Prairies and made their way to Everett, Lynden, Seattle, and Oak Harbor, Washington. Every Dutch settlement in western Canada seemed to contribute at least one man or family to the pioneering efforts of the Dutch in Washington.[16]

Conditions improved in the western provinces by the mid-1920's because of the organization of the Wheat Pool in 1924, sufficient rainfall, the stabilization of prices, and the expansion of crop yields due to new farming techniques and grain varieties. An upturn in the national economy, which began in 1925, also promised a return to good times. As a result, successful single farmers, who had returned to the Netherlands to find wives, also recruited farm hands to work in the Dutch communities. While there was little cheap land available, there was plenty of farm work for able young men. As long as the crops were good and the prices steady, these settlements continued to attract immigrants.

Lack of land forced the sons of homesteaders and new immigrants to look to new areas of settlement. One promising district lay west of Lacombe in central Alberta. This area, in the more humid and forested park belt, was suitable for mixed farming and could support grain, grass, cattle, and hogs. But it was still wooded and needed to be cleared. Settlers were recruited in the Netherlands by the Calvinist Emigration Society and arrived in 1927, 1928, and 1929. Working as local farm hands and clearing part-time, they began the task of breaking and draining the wetlands. The settlement process was slow and painful; initial sales were small, and until families arrived the life was lonesome. By 1930, a small beginning, but a determined one, promised a good future for the Lacombe settlers. The early establishment of religious services and the desire to organize a Christian Reformed church did much to tie the Dutch settlers together and helped them weather the difficult times.[17]

The Dutch communities in Edmonton and Neerlandia had grown during the war years but, like Nobleford, their development slowed in the 1920's. Jobs for non-agricultural immigrants were scarce in the cities and while farm jobs were available, homestead or cheap land was in short supply. The Neerlandia settlement had expanded to its full limit by the 1920's and many homesteaders' sons were forced to look elsewhere for land. Some of them went to the Lacombe settlement while others examined opportunities in northern Saskatchewan and Alberta. Such conditions often meant that many young single men, particularly immigrants, held farm jobs in the summer and drifted to the cities of the West Coast in the winter. Many families, unable to find permanent positions, turned either to the cities or to the more secure life in Ontario.

In spite of the difficulties, each year brought a new wave of immigrants to the West. To some, the temperate climate of coastal British Columbia promised to be a haven from the extremes of prairie temperatures. Single men and families sought jobs as craftsmen and labourers, but the majority worked on the farms surrounding the city of Vancouver. By 1929 a Christian Reformed church and an immigrant aid society were established there, but the scarcity of cheap land discouraged any great rush to the area. The Dutch community continued to grow, however, and by 1931, 1,936 people of Dutch origin were known to reside in Vancouver. It was to remain a final Canadian refuge for those who could not succeed elsewhere.[18]

THE THIRTIES

In the fall of 1929 commodity prices began to decline across Canada. The western wheat farmer, already faced with low crop yields, was forced to sell his wheat at steadily diminishing prices. The 1930 price of sixty-four cents a bushel spelled the beginning of the end for those farmers whose profit margin was too small to allow them to meet their debts. Most farmers had seen hard times before, and many clung to the hope of an economic upturn. The Canadian government seemed to share that hope and continued to permit recruitment of agricultural immigrants in the spring of 1930.

The actual demand for such immigrants, however, had significantly decreased. The farmers in the East as well as in the West were in the process of retrenchment and fewer jobs were available. The situation discouraged potential Dutch immigrants, and only 788 persons, as compared to the previous year's 1,458, came to Canada in 1930.[19] By August, 1930, the Canadian government realized that not only were immigrants having difficulty finding jobs but they were also taking jobs away from Canadians. The government responded by limiting admission of immigrants to dependants of Canadian residents and to those who had sufficient capital to begin farming immediately upon arrival.[20]

The limitation of immigration had far-reaching effects in both the Netherlands and Canada. The new government regulations effectively barred the immigration of assisted immigrants and farm hands – those who had made up the bulk of the immigration in the past. The actual number of immigrants who could fulfil the Canadian requirement quickly declined. The best available figures on Dutch immigration to Canada indicate a steady decline in numbers from 269 in 1931 to 148 in 1934. Most of those who came during this period were dependants of Dutch Canadians because those who had capital were hesitant to change the known in Holland for the unknown of Canada. The number of immigrants increased in 1935 to 208, fell in 1936 to 192, and then began a slow climb to 411 in 1939. The outbreak of the Second World War forced the number down to 238 in 1940 and, for the time being, effectively ended Dutch immigration to Canada. The total number of immigrants for the ten-year period, 1930-1940, was 3,184.[21]

During the depression years the government continued to restrict immigration primarily to those who could be supported by relatives or to immigrants who had enough capital to begin farming and look after themselves. In the first years of the depression, this latter group was told by the Canadian government that the only areas suitable for settlement were in New Brunswick and Nova Scotia.[22] The federal and provincial governments believed that Dutch farmers could put abandoned farms in those provinces back into production. An investigation was initiated by the Netherlands Emigration Foundation and it was concluded that such settlement would be difficult because of the condition of the abandoned land, poor transportation facilities, and poor prices. It was further noted that those who had property or goods in the Netherlands would find it difficult to dispose of them. Because of these problems, and because of a lack of interest on the part of the Dutch citizens, the idea of settlement in the Maritimes was discouraged by the NEF.[23]

As the economic crisis deepened and unemployment grew, the Canadian government became increasingly unwilling to accept any assisted immigrants at all, and in January of 1934 all entry by such persons was prohibited. This meant that even those immigrants who had part of the $1,000 settlement money the government demanded could not borrow the remainder from the Netherlands Emigration Foundation in order to settle in Canada. As economic conditions began to improve in Canada after 1936, the government reopened the immigration door somewhat. In 1937, in addition to qualified farmers with capital and dependants, all people who had sufficient capital to begin their own businesses and who met the other requirements of the immigration laws were to be permitted entry to Canada. The Canadian government also expanded the eligible categories of immigrants to include married sons and daughters and grandchildren of farm families in Canada.[24]

To give more business to Canadian railways, the Canadian consular officials in Holland were instructed to give immigration certificates only to those people who came to Canada under the auspices of the CNR or CPR. Any potential emigrants who applied to the Netherlands Emigration Foundation were given information on conditions in Canada and referred to the freight representative of the CNR. This agent provided the emigrants with transportation on the Holland-America Line. The CPR freight agent booked passage for his applicants on CPR ships.[25]

The declaration of war against Germany by the Dominion of Canada on September 10, 1939, threatened to put an end to immigration altogether. Passage rates on neutral ships immediately jumped 40 per cent, and the dangers of submarines and mines made the passage to Canada hazardous. The Canadian government, no doubt thinking about future war needs, continued to encourage the recruitment of Dutch farmers. Interest in emigration escalated in the Netherlands as conditions grew worse in Europe. Among others, a few Dutch Jews, with sufficient capital for the move, sought the safety of a far-distant Canada. Emigrants continued to leave the Netherlands for Canada until Holland's precarious neutrality was ended by the German invasion of May 10, 1940.[26]

The Dutch immigrants who came to Canada in 1929 and 1930 barely had time to adjust to Canadian life before the economic conditions began to worsen. Those who were fortunate enough to have a job tried to hold on to it. Since most were hired hands, their futures were entirely dependent on the sale of their employers' produce. Somehow the vast majority stayed employed and off the welfare rolls. Those who were unfortunate enough to have to apply for help found that getting on municipal or city welfare was not all that simple and that non-citizens receiving such aid were liable to deportation if local officials believed they would become permanently dependent on public charity.

The classification of an alien as a "public charge" by local officials quickly attracted the attention of immigration officials. An investigation was undertaken to determine the immigrant's potential for employment, his skills, his personal property, and any responsibility he might have for other persons resident in Canada. Of the 201 Dutch immigrants deported between 1930 and 1935, over half were members of families. Sixty per cent of the deportees were classified as public charges while the rest were deported for medical, civil, or criminal causes or because they were accompanying deported persons.

The Dutch experience with deportation was not unique among immigrant groups. It is evident that deportations were highest during the worst years of economic crisis and reached their peak in 1932. The Canadian government seems to have consistently used its powers to deport immigrants it regarded as a financial liability.

Those Dutch immigrants who wished to avoid deportation from Canada made their way to the consul general for the Netherlands at Montreal. Some wanted money to get on their feet again, but most asked for repatriation. Consul General J.A. Schuurman had received such requests before the depression, but they now began to overwhelm him and drain his available funds. His immediate reaction was to turn against the semi-official emigration societies and blame them for the poor selection of immigrants. Regarding them as responsible, he asked that they provide remuneration for his work. The NEF carefully documented the cases presented by the consul general, disavowed any responsibility, and correctly laid the blame for the poor selection on the shoulders of the transportation agents. Schuurman doubted that complaints to the Canadian government would have any results. The transportation companies had, in the past, refused to listen to the protests of the Netherlands Emigration League against the agents' activities. In spite of literally dozens of well-documented cases, which proved that immigrants had been lured by deceptive and illusory promises, the companies had not put an end to these practices. The Dutch could only conclude that the work was too profitable for them to order the agents to desist and that the

Canadian government was influenced by the transportation companies to look the other way. Nothing remained but for the Ministry of Foreign Affairs and its consul general in Canada to try to help as many indigent and distressed immigrants as possible, at its own cost. At least the NEF and its representatives could be counted on to help. The decision not to abandon the immigrants was to have important consequences for the Holland Marsh settlement in Ontario.[27]

HOLLAND MARSH

The settlement in the Holland Marsh typifies the reaction of most Dutch immigrants to the challenges of the decade. They not only struggled for survival but fought to make themselves economically secure and financially independent in a harsh and demanding new era.

In spite of bad economic conditions, neither the Netherlands Emigration Foundation nor John Snor of Hamilton, a part-time antique dealer and their part-time Canadian representative, gave up hope of continued immigration. Fearing that single-family settlement would be too difficult, they began to examine the possibilities of a colony type of development. A colony of immigrants with money would permit the exchange of work, the sharing of implements, and the pooling of resources. Perhaps more important, a colony would promote a sense of unity and solidarity that would help the settlers withstand the hardships.

John Snor looked for some sort of opportunity that would appeal to Dutch farmers. He thought he had found it in Holland Marsh, a boggy area located at the outlet of Lake Simcoe, twenty-five miles north of Toronto. Although much of the marsh was overgrown with bushes and trees, drainage canals had already been built by private investors and the deep black soil was eminently suitable for vegetable growing. Even though some of the area had been brought into production between 1900 and 1930, plenty of unreclaimed land was still available. A number of truck farmers, including a few Dutchmen, had already established farms there and were growing vegetables for the Toronto market.

Snor believed that a settlement of Dutch farmers with sufficient capital could succeed in this area, and he sought the aid of the NEF and the Canadian Department of Immigration and Colonization. In 1932 the NEF sent D.C. Peters, the Washington agricultural attaché, to investigate the possibilities. Peters urged that the Holland Marsh be seriously considered for immigrants who came to Canada with the required $1,000. His report and Snor's recommendations and plans were closely examined by both the Dutch and the Canadians and, with no objections being registered by the Canadian provincial or federal governments, the NEF decided to recruit immigrants for the Holland Marsh.[28]

The recruitment campaign was a dismal failure; no applicants came forward in the Netherlands with sufficient capital to begin farming in the Holland Marsh. Also, the ownership of the land was in dispute and claims and counterclaims were continually being filed in Canadian courts. Furthermore, the vegetable trade was in the hands of Toronto middlemen, who levied a 12 per cent handling charge on all marketed vegetables and completely controlled distribution. None of this augured well for the independent farmer, whose only alternative lay in co-operative storage and marketing facilities he could not afford to build.[29]

Reluctantly, the NEF came to the conclusion that the settlement plans should be abandoned. The lack of clear titles was a distinct deterrent, as was the Canadian government's decision to prohibit assisted immigration of any kind. Local objections to the settlement, due to growing unemployment, had given the Canadian government second thoughts about the wisdom of encouraging such developments in a time of economic distress. Finally, Snor's conflict with the NEF about his salary and alleged shortcomings in bookkeeping led to a complete break and his discharge as a representative of the NEF in 1934.[30]

In the meantime, Snor had investigated the possibility of developing his own settlement for Canadian farmers and Dutch immigrants already resident in Canada. In the spring of 1934, he made an agreement with the Canada Company, one of the large landowners on the Marsh, to purchase a plot of land, reclaim it, build houses on it, and encourage development. He began the slow task of clearing land, repairing the drainage ditches, and making the land ready for farming. This was all done at his own expense, with the hope that the sale of the farm plots would reimburse his time and expenses and result in some profit. Snor spent all of 1934 preparing the land and building homes. The response from settlers was not great, however, and only six families, Dutch and Canadian, purchased land from him. Snor faced the grim spectre of bankruptcy and desperately sought a way out of his financial predicament.[31]

He discovered an opportunity to salvage his finances and his plans in the Relief Land Settlement Agreement of 1932. Under this agreement the Dominion and provincial governments "supported programs to establish would-be reliefers on farmlands in Canada's unsettled regions. In theory the money spent to support a city family on relief in one year could make the family self-sustaining on a farm."[32] Snor felt that such a program was ready-made for the relief of hard-working Dutch immigrants who faced destitution or deportation.

After negotiating with the Dominion government, the province of Ontario, and the Netherlands government (which was concerned to avoid the repatriation of failed emigrants), he secured their agreement to finance the settlement of would-be Dutch immigrant reliefers on the lands he owned in the Holland Marsh. Each of the governments agreed to contribute $200 per family to a general fund to be used to pay the initial expenses of the settlers. Snor was designated as the trustee of the fund. Under the Relief Land Settlement Agreement settlement funds normally came from federal, provincial, and municipal governments. On the urging of J.A. Schuurman, the Dutch consul general at Montreal, the Dutch government decided to contribute the municipality's share because King Township had declared its inability to do so. The NEF was directed by the Dutch government to pay the municipality's share for those of its assisted immigrants who had come in previous years and were now in financial difficulties and who wanted to settle in the Holland Marsh under the Relief Land Settlement Agreement.[33]

In order to have some supervision over the project, the Dutch government retained John Snor as its representative at a salary of $90 a month. He settled sixteen Dutch families on the Marsh in the spring of 1935. Each family received $600 of credit, five acres of land, a small garden strip, and a house. Taxes on the land were to be paid directly to the local township and land payments to the Bank of Commerce in Bradford to reimburse Snor and the Canada Company. Settlers were permitted to spend their credit for seed, food, and implements. This small investment, it was hoped, would lead to economic self-sufficiency in the coming years because the first year's crop would pay the taxes and the initial land payment and provide seed money for the following year.[34]

By 1938 it was clear that the initial working capital of $600 per settler had been too small to give the settler a fighting chance. Practically all of the farmers had grown large cash crops in order to pay their debts, but they had been unable to produce enough food for themselves. They were therefore forced to buy their staples from merchants in Bradford, and the continual drain of cash meant that there was none to reinvest in the purchase of trucks or the establishment of a marketing co-operative. Without transportation or distribution facilities, they were forced to sell their produce to Toronto jobbers and accept low prices. The result was that township taxes were not paid and payments on the land were in arrears. Necessities, such as food and clothing, were increasingly in short supply. The local Christian Reformed congregation, which had been organized by Calvinist settlers, appealed to congregations in the United States for aid, and some clothing and gifts did arrive to help the settlers.[35]

Relations between Snor and the settlers also deteriorated over the years. In the beginning, in honour of Snor's leading role in the settlement, the settlers had named their small community Ansnorveld, but by 1938 he had lost their trust and respect. Snor continually complained to the settlers about their failure to pay township taxes. He feared that the township would eventually seize their land for tax sales and that he would lose his investment.[36]

The six families who had bought land directly from Snor also had problems with him. Some had done reasonably well and had been able to pay him for their property. They expected that he would reimburse the Canada Company and free their titles to the land. Instead, Snor had allegedly appropriated the money for his own use. Somehow he managed to balance one interest against the other and kept his head above water, but in so doing he enraged everyone from the settlers to the provincial authorities.

Snor's manipulation of the funds also distressed the Dutch government because they were concerned about all the Dutch residents on the Marsh. They threatened to cut off his salary if he made any moves against those settlers who were behind in their payments and eventually fired Snor in May of 1939. Snor threatened to foreclose immediately upon his dismissal but was dissuaded from such action by the realization that he would jeopardize his investment if the bank called in his loan. He decided, instead, to wait, and the settlers remained on the Marsh.

In spite of everything, the Holland Marsh experiment was not an entire failure. It was obvious that many relief settlers were no better off economically than they had been before the venture was begun. Nevertheless, the Dutch government supported the settlement because it believed that the Holland Marsh might be a good destination if emigration increased in the coming years. From a social and psychological viewpoint, the settlement had been fairly successful. Sixteen families without hope or substance had fought their way to some sort of personal victory. The consul general in Montreal observed that "The families on the Marsh don't want to leave, no matter how difficult things may be, perhaps only because they value their personal relations. They find it '*gezellig*' [convivial]."[37] The sense of community, with its inherent support and protection, far outweighed the economic disadvantages of the settlement. Snor's manipulations, economic distress, and the monopoly of the vegetable jobbers only served to strengthen the bonds of unity that permitted the survival of the Dutch settlement on the Holland Marsh.

The outbreak of the war and the resultant rise in the prices and demand of agricultural products eventually brought returns which guaranteed Snor's investment and the success of the settlement.

As economic conditions improved in Canada in the late 1930's, the Canadian railway companies attempted to reawaken Dutch interest in emigration. The Canadian Pacific Railway sought to sell lands in Stormont County, Ontario, and produced an illustrated brochure with descriptions of farms and pictures of homes and barns. The Canadian National began discussions with the NEF in 1937 concerning the recruitment of immigrants for group settlements in Nova Scotia, New Brunswick, the Prairie provinces, and British Columbia. It was especially interested in finding settlers for land along the railway line to Prince Rupert in central British Columbia, which had been completed in 1914. The land had few settlers and the company believed that Dutch settlers would be suitable as pioneers. To recruit the immigrants they turned to Jacob Prins of Edmonton, Alberta.

Jacob Prins and his family had emigrated to Canada from Andijk, North Holland, in March of 1927. He had become a successful farmer in the Edmonton area and an important member of the Christian Reformed community. He worried about the dispersion of the Calvinist immigrants and the resulting loss of their faith and, before the depression curtailed his work, had aided a number of immigrants in their trek to Canada. Increasing inquiries from Holland in the years after 1935 once again involved Prins in the immigration movement. He settled a number of families at Lacombe and strengthened the Dutch settlement there.[38]

Mr. and Mrs. John Kuyten and son, Frank, Strathmore, Alberta, ca. 1912.
(Courtesy Glenbow Archives, Calgary, NA 3503-9)

Dutch immigrants proceeding to the Grand Trunk Railway ferry, Quebec, ca. 1900.
(Courtesy Directie voor de Emigratie, The Hague)

Mr. and Mrs. Luite Visscher, New Holland, Alberta, 1915.
(Courtesy Glenbow Archives, Calgary, NA 4520-3)

Private Kornelius Gerrit Devries, 50th Battalion, 21st Reserve, C.E.F., ca. 1914-18.
(Courtesy Glenbow Archives, Calgary, NA 3007-1)

Janus Bestebroer's sod shack and Netherlands Transatlantic Mortgage Co. office, Morse, Saskatchewan, ca. 1915. (Courtesy D. Hoogeveen, Regina)

Van Wyk home, Didsbury, Alberta, 1915. (Courtesy Mrs. H. Van Wyk, Calgary)

Congregation of First Reformed Church, New Holland, Alberta, 1924.
(Courtesy Glenbow Archives, Calgary, NA 4520-10)

The arrival of a group of Netherlanders in Winnipeg, 1920's.
(Courtesy Directie voor de Emigratie, The Hague)

Janus Bestebroer and Mr. Droogleever-Fortuyn, Teulon, Manitoba, 1920's.
(Courtesy D. Hoogeveen, Regina)

Students and teachers at New Holland school, New Holland, Alberta, 1921.
(Courtesy Glenbow Archives, Calgary, NA 4520-5)

Holland farmers placed by the Central Emigration Foundation Holland, 1st Annual Picnic,
La Salle Park, 1927. (Courtesy Directie voor de Emigratie, The Hague)

Symen Van Wyk, Alberta cowboy and ranger, Nordegg, ca. 1930.
(Courtesy Mrs. H. Van Wyk, Calgary)

Corporal Bernard M. Mason, Strathmore, Alberta, and Wilhelmina E. de Weerd,
Heemskerk, North Holland, Heemskerk, April 10, 1946.
(Courtesy Mr. and Mrs. B. Mason, Calgary)

The furniture crate of the Bezeuyen family, Den Helder, 1951.
(Courtesy J. Bezeuyen, St. Catharines)

Departure at the quay, The Netherlands, 1940's and 1950's.
(Courtesy Directie voor de Emigratie, The Hague)

Waiting for a ride to church, Beamsville, Ontario, 1949.
(Courtesy M. Ganzevoort, Niagara-on-the-Lake)

The Van Eek and Bezeuyen families arriving at St. Catharines, from Quebec City,
April, 1951. (Courtesy J. Bezeuyen, St. Catharines)

J.C. Damen on the Groote Beer *on the way to Canada, 1953.*
(Courtesy J.C. Damen, Penticton)

Hoeing beets in southern Alberta, 1950's.
(Courtesy the Stuyvenberg family, St. Catharines)

First home in Canada, Coaldale, Alberta, 1950's.
(Courtesy the Stuyvenberg family, St. Catharines)

The Hamoen family and their first car (1933 Dodge), Clinton, Ontario, 1952.
(Courtesy the Hamoen family, St. Catharines)

J.C. Damen at the Alcan plant, Kitimat, B.C., ca. 1954. (Courtesy J.C. Damen, Penticton)

Maranatha Christian Reformed Church, old (1951) and new, St. Catharines, Ontario, 1954.
(Courtesy the Bezeuyen family, St. Catharines)

Departing for Canada, Schiphol, The Netherlands, April 20, 1955.
(Courtesy J. Lowensteyn, Rosemere)

His frequent contacts with the CNR led the company to offer him a free trip to Holland in the spring of 1937 to interview prospective immigrants. On his return he was given a guided tour of the Bulkley Valley in the Houston area of British Columbia to explore the possibility of settling Dutch farmers with capital. He then returned to Holland to recruit vegetable growers and seedmen from his native town of Andijk. In the spring of 1938 he brought back with him two settlers who were to report back to others in Andijk about the prospects for settlement. They decided that opportunities looked good and urged the others to come to the Bulkley Valley.[39]

During 1939, families came from the Netherlands and from other parts of Canada to settle the Bulkley Valley, and by the end of October the community had grown to twelve families and a couple of individuals. Although conditions were difficult, the settlers were supported in their endeavours by the community feeling and the establishment of a Christian Reformed church in 1939. By the spring of 1940, the settlement seemed fairly well established and on its way to continuing growth. The invasion of the Netherlands destroyed any hope of continued immigration or financial support from home and forced the community to live on its own resources.

NOTES

1. "Emigration to Middle Canada," *Handelsberichten*, 563, p. 2, NESC, GAI.
2. Hartland, *De Geschiedenis*, p. 155; T.H. De Meester to the Ministry of External Affairs, 23 March 1926, NESC, GAI.
3. P. Snoek to the Netherlands Emigration League, 11 November 1924, NESC, GAI.
4. Monteyn, "Report on Conditions," pp. 1-24; Consul General Schuurman to the Ministry of External Affairs, 18 July 1927, NESC, GAI.
5. F.G. De Veer to the Netherlands Emigration League, 10 July 1924; F.G. De Veer to the Central Emigration Foundation Holland, 19 March 1925, NESC, GAI.
6. *Voorwaarts*, 8 July 1924, NESC, GAI.
7. J. Snor to the Netherlands Emigration Foundation, 27 April 1932, NESC, GAI.
8. Consul General J.A. Schuurman to the Ministry of External Affairs, 17 May 1930, NESC, GAI.
9. E. Sullivan to the Netherlands Consul, Toronto, 7 July 1927, NESC, GAI.
10. *Winschoter Courant*, 1 February 1930; *Arnhemsche Courant*, 4 February 1928, NESC, GAI.
11. J. Snor to the Netherlands Emigration Foundation, 7 April 1932, NESC, GAI.
12. Consistory and Congregation Minutes of the Canadian Christian Reformed churches, Heritage Hall Archives, Calvin College, Grand Rapids, Michigan.
13. *De Standaard*, 2 November 1929, NESC, GAI; Martha Knapp to author, 13 February 1973.
14. L. Van Riemesdyk to the Central Emigration Foundation Holland, 8 September 1926, NESC, GAI.

15. H.F. 't Hooft to author, 13 December 1972.
16. J.J. Leys, *Nederlandsche Kolonisten*, pp. 25, 34.
17. *Friesch Dagblad*, 28 December 1927, NESC, GAI; H.J. ten Hove to author, 17 October, 11 December 1972.
18. *De Standaard*, 21 February 1929, NESC, GAI; *Census of Canada*, 1931, p. 296.
19. Hartland, *De Geschiedenis*, p. 162.
20. Ministry of External Affairs to the Central Emigration Foundation Holland, 20 August 1930 [Telephone transcript], NESC, GAI.
21. Hartland, *De Geschiedenis*, p. 162.
22. The Netherlands Emigration Foundation to the Ministry of Social Affairs, 11 May 1937, NESC, GAI.
23. D.C. Peters, "Report on the Visit to Nova Scotia, 1931," NESC, GAI.
24. The Netherlands Emigration Foundation to the Ministry of Social Affairs, 11 May 1937; J.A.A. Hartland, "The Outlook of Emigration and its Organization, 1937"; The Netherlands Emigration Foundation to the Friesian Calvinist Colonization Society, 14 October 1938, NESC, GAI.
25. The Netherlands Emigration Foundation to the Friesian Calvinist Colonization Society, 6 June 1939, N.E.F. to Ministry of Social Affairs, 18 July 1939, NESC, GAI.
26. The Netherlands Emigration Foundation to the Friesian Calvinist Colonization Society, 7 October, 20 December 1939, NESC, GAI.
27. The Netherlands Emigration Foundation to the Ministry of Labour, Trade and Commerce, 30 March 1932; O.D. Skelton to Consul General J.A. Schuurman, 12 October 1933; Department of Immigration and Colonization, "Investigations Report," 19 November 1939, NESC, GAI.
28. John Snor to F.C. Blair, 29 December 1931, Department of Immigration and Colonization Files, PAC; Hartland, *De Geschiedenis*, p. 93.
29. Hartland, *De Geschiedenis*, pp. 93-99, 162.
30. The Netherlands Emigration Foundation (Winnipeg) to Manson and May Company, 9 February 1934; The Netherlands Emigration Foundation (Winnipeg), 30 August 1934, NESC, GAI.
31. The Netherlands Emigration Foundation to L. Van Riemesdyk, 1 March 1933, NESC, GAI; Memorandum from F.C. Blair to the Minister of Immigration and Colonization, 10 August 1934, PAC.
32. L.M. Grayson and M. Bliss, eds., *The Wretched of Canada* (1971), pp. xv-xvi.
33. Memorandum from F.C. Blair to the Minister of Immigration and Colonization, 3 December 1934, Department of Immigration and Colonization Files, PAC; the Netherlands Emigration Foundation (The Hague) to the Netherlands Emigration Foundation (Winnipeg), 24 March 1935, NESC, GAI. The final agreement for the relief of settlers on the Holland Marsh stipulated that each family was to receive $600. Two hundred dollars each was given by the government of Canada, the Ontario provincial government, and the Dutch government (the last being the municipal share under the Relief Land Settlement Agreement of 1932).

34. Consul General J.A. Schuurman to the Ministry of External Affairs, 9 December 1938; Ministry of External Affairs, "Consul's Report on the Holland Marsh," 21 October 1938, p. 8, NESC, GAI.
35. Consul General J.A. Schuurman to the Ministry of External Affairs, 9 December 1938, NESC, GAI; interview with Mrs. G. Kamp by author.
36. Ministry of External Affairs, "Consul's Report on the Holland Marsh," pp. 1-2, NESC, GAI.
37. Consul General J.A. Schuurman to the Ministry of External Affairs, 9 December 1938, NESC, GAI.
38. H.J. ten Hove to author, 11 December 1972.
39. Consul General J.A. Schuurman to Ministry of External Affairs, 23 March 1939, NESC, GAI.

PART THREE

The Flood and Ebb, 1939–1980

FIVE

The Second World War and Its Aftermath

Canada's declaration of war on Germany in September, 1939, brought vast changes to a country that had suffered ten years of searing economic depression. Unemployed men and surplus production were now redirected to the war effort and for the first time in a decade the economic picture began to brighten. Dutch Canadians from all walks of life, but particularly from the agricultural sector, were an active part of this redeployment and change.

By 1939 a new generation of Canadian Dutch had grown up in Canada. They were wholly committed to the country and the past resentments of their parents played little part in their loyalty to the Dominion of Canada as a member of the British Commonwealth of Nations. The invasion of the Netherlands in the spring of 1940 by the Germans and the destruction of France and possible capitulation of England simply sharpened their support for the destruction of the Nazi hordes. Dutch Canadians, like their compatriots, saw their role as the producers of goods and foodstuffs to fuel the military engines of Canada and England. Whether labourers, factory workers, clerks, grain growers in southern Alberta, truck-farmers in the Holland Marsh, or fruit growers in the Niagara Peninsula, they were united in a common cause that would lead to the defeat of the enemy and the liberation of the Netherlands.

The new markets and demands for goods and services affected every Dutch Canadian. Young men worked on farms and in factories and others enlisted in the military forces. The Dutch communities across the country contributed to and benefited from the mobilization of men and resources. Immigrant women took their place alongside their men in the field as well as the factory and made as great a contribution as possible.

Beyond aiding the war effort there was little that the immigrants could do about the situation in their homeland. Although a few refugees from Holland and its overseas possessions were to come to Canada, immigration came to a virtual standstill. One of the most prominent arrivals was Crown Princess Juliana, heir to the Dutch throne, who with her family sought asylum in Canada while Queen Wilhelmina stayed in England to give moral support to her subjects across the Channel. In 1942, Dutch Canadians welcomed the entry of the United States into the war and hoped for an early end to the war. The invasion of the continent in 1944 and Canadian military activity in the southern Netherlands by the autumn of that year seemed to make all their past efforts worthwhile. The crowning touch was the liberation of their homeland in May of 1945 by Canadian troops.

During the war years the Dutch communities had grown significantly in terms of production, land development, and the demands for labour. Believing that such growth would continue in the post-war period and that the Netherlands would be in economic shambles, Dutch Canadians viewed immigration with the highest of hopes. While the first letters home to the Netherlands after the war were primarily to determine the fate of family and friends, they quickly turned to the possibilities Canada held for their loved ones. The situation in the Netherlands caused such appeals to fall on fertile ground.

THE DUTCH PERSPECTIVE

The spring of 1945 ushered in a difficult decade for the Dutch nation. The Nazis had been crushed, the country liberated, but the cost of five long years of war was all too apparent. Thousands of acres of land lay inundated by seawater, despoiled by the German attempt to halt the inevitable advance of the Allies. Ruined cities, shattered transportation networks, devastated industrial centres, and a barely functioning economy dulled the taste of victory. Reconstruction, self-denial, and a harnessing of the national will would be necessary to put the Netherlands back on its feet.

There were, however, things to rejoice about. Freedom, after the years of occupation, was simply an indescribable joy. There was no longer a need to watch what one said and to whom. The beloved Queen Wilhelmina and her family returned from exile carrying with them Margriet, the Canadian-born daughter of Juliana. The liberating armies, particularly the Canadians, were friendly and helpful, and their overabundant supplies of food, chewing gum, and chocolate promised an end to the shortages and starvation of the previous winter. There was hope, as well as a stubborn belief that somehow Holland would put itself back together again.

It was soon clear that the Dutch government had no instant answers to the problems that plagued the economy, tied as it was to the whole western European economic system, which now lay in the doldrums among the wrecked machinery. The population growth of the Netherlands had continued despite economic and political turmoil and many felt that their small country would never be able to absorb the growing numbers. Full employment, social mobility, economic advancement, the purchase of land, or the extension of farm acreage seemed impossible given the economic and social problems.

Others resented the return of a full-blown bureaucracy, which once again, as in the pre-war years, re-established its position with myriad forms and bales of papers. Some likened it to a second occupation, only this time the enemy was their own countrymen and there was little justification for revolt.

Perhaps, although few would admit it, there was a secret longing for the type of freedom that had existed during the occupation. Then the enemy was known, and one was justified in disobedience and in attempts to wreck the system. More importantly, then there had been a unity and cohesiveness in Dutch society. It seemed as if all parts, the right, the left, Protestants, Catholics, workers and employers, north and south, had put aside the old quarrels to face the enemy. Now they were divided again, back in the old system of compromise for survival. It was once again necessary to surrender personal freedom for society to survive, and many felt thwarted and restless.

In the immediate post-war years political events throughout the world convinced others that Europe would once again become the cockpit of another war. The predictable fall of the eastern European countries under the colossus of communism seemed to threaten western Europe with a red tide that would sweep all before it. A significant number of people began to look for a place to escape, far from this scene of impending disaster.

The problems that were to spur on the massive movement of people from the Netherlands in the immediate post-war years had long plagued the Dutch people and their government. Overpopulation, unemployment, and the limited amount of arable land had presented critical choices even before the turn of the century. Those who had preached emigration as a solution prior to the Second World War had met with little success, either in promoting emigration or in solving the problems. Now these same problems had been exacerbated by the war and cried out for an answer.

Was emigration such an answer? The pre-war experience had indicated the greatest hindrance to emigration was not lack of ability or the lack of suitable prospective emigrants, but simply that few wanted to leave the comforts of hearth and home. For good or ill the average Dutchman loved his country, his social life, his family, all that made him a Dutchman, and he was reluctant to give this up. It seemed that only the grave or the most critical conditions could move him.

The pessimism with which the Dutch viewed their future simply reflected the opinions held in government circles. There the pessimism was supported by figures and statistics: over 500,000 acres of land had been inundated by salt water, a condition that would retard crop production for years; 4 per cent of all housing had been destroyed; factories had been bombed or destroyed and many had their machinery looted by the retreating German forces. Replacement parts for the remaining machinery were unobtainable as many of the spare parts had to come from the manufacturers whose factories now lay destroyed in Germany. Furthermore, Germany had been one of Holland's most important export clients in the pre-war period and that country, now in ruins, was a market of no consequence.

This bleak picture was made worse by the ever-increasing population, which at over nine million made the Netherlands the most densely populated country in western Europe. That in itself was not a serious problem as long as the economic possibilities continued to grow apace and offer new jobs for the expanding work force. While there had been a slow decline in the birthrate during the 1930's, the death rate had also declined. To complicate things further, the birthrate had declined in urban areas, particularly among professionals and workers, but there had not been a similar decline among the rural population. Religion played an important part, as Roman Catholic and orthodox Calvinists had the highest rate of fertility. It was clear that the greatest population pressure and its resulting problems could be expected in the countryside among the Roman Catholics and orthodox Calvinists.

Almost from the moment of liberation, the Dutch government began to examine the opportunities for the mass movement of people out of the country. The Ministry of Foreign Affairs requested reports from its overseas embassies in Canada, the United States, South America, South Africa, Australia, and New Zealand as to the possibilities for settlement. The answers were not encouraging. Many of the countries were in the process of troop demobilization, finding employment for their own people, and redirecting their wartime industries to peacetime production.

Their general attitude was that it was much too soon after the war to think of immigration and that some time would have to pass before it would even be considered. As well, the United States had a fixed quota of 3,136 Dutch immigrants per year and South Africa had little need for agricultural workers who would cost more than the blacks. The most persistent obstacle, however, was the lack of transportation, as there were few ships to carry emigrants even if countries had been open to them.

MAKING UP OUR MINDS

The critical problems of overpopulation, unemployment, and lack of arable land created difficulties that produced a society under great stress. Clearly an outlet had to be found for the building frustration that affected so many. The spark that ignited the fire of emigration came from Canada.

The liberation of the Netherlands by Canadian forces had a significant effect on the Dutch. The difficult struggles in 1944-45 to push out the entrenched Germans, and the subsequent losses of Canadian soldiers in those battles, were deeply appreciated by the Dutch citizens. They equated the return of their freedom with the arrival of the Canadians and as a result welcomed them into their homes when temporary billeting was needed.

It is also clear that, while communication was difficult, the Dutch were generally impressed by the behaviour, good manners, and generosity of their liberators. People who had lived with shortages since 1929, and more particularly since the beginning of the war, were overwhelmed by the apparent affluence of the Canadian soldiers. They reasoned that any country that could supply the incalculable number of necessities of an army on the march must be tremendously wealthy, for suddenly there seemed to be an abundance of food, candy, and even razor blades and cigarettes. The fraternization between soldiers and civilians, which eventually led to marriages, helped to cement close ties. A family that saw its daughter depart for Canada as one of 1,886 war brides gave thought to the possibility of life overseas.

Another and perhaps more important influence on emigration was the re-established contact with relatives and friends in Canada. Although the cost had been high in loneliness and difficult labour, the Dutch Canadians were relatively affluent. Certainly compared to those they had left behind, they had opportunities their European brothers longed for. As the difficult conditions of their relatives and friends became clear, Dutch Canadians responded by sending packages of coffee and tea and other goods. Soon letters arrived urging emigration to Canada. Promises of jobs and housing were enhanced by grand descriptions of the possibilities that existed for those who had the will to work and succeed. Few promised gold on the streets, but many remarked that land was cheap and jobs plentiful, particularly in agriculture. They wrote to tell of the Canadian soldiers who, once demobilized, were reluctant to return to the farm and agricultural jobs they had left at enlistment. Farm labourers were becoming increasingly scarce and many farms were being abandoned to the old, whose work years would soon be coming to an end. A man who desired to work, better yet a family with strong boys and girls, would have an almost assured chance of success. While the initial years would be hard, by pooling their money, working shares, or working away from the farm for extra income they could accumulate the capital to buy land, equipment, and a home.[1]

It was an opportunity too good to ignore, and it came from those they trusted – their relatives. Suddenly the long lines, the frustration with government bureaucrats, the lack of freedom, the fear of communism and war could all be swept aside. There would be no more shortages, no more living with mother and father, no more renting ten hectares and putting the profit in someone else's pocket. The Canadian government did not regulate and control everything in minute detail; petty officialdom had little chance of survival in a land that was so big that one of the Great Lakes would easily swallow up all of the Netherlands. In Canada large families were an asset, not a hindrance, and work and effort were rewarded. Every child could be assured of an inheritance, which in the Netherlands was only within the expectations of wealthy landowners.

The idea of emigration became a kind of fever, an exhilarating enthusiasm, a compulsion that could not be denied. While the older family members hesitated, figuring the odds and generally being negative or acting as devil's advocates, many young men and women gave themselves completely over to the prospect of emigration. Unconvinced parents found their children rebelling for the first time and were faced with the threat of being abandoned by children determined to go. One child influenced another, and eventually, to save at least a modicum of authority and family discipline, the parents surrendered. More often than not, once the decision had been made, even they became enthralled by the possibilities.

In some sense the choice of Canada as a destination was no choice at all. Those who felt compelled to emigrate were naturally drawn to those places where their relatives and fellow countrymen had had some success. Canada was one of the few countries in the immediate post-war period prepared to accept Dutch immigrants. South America had only a few small Dutch colonies and life in the jungle held little appeal for those from the temperate flatlands of the Dutch countryside. South Africa was a country in which large amounts of capital were necessary to establish a farm and most immigrants had little. New Zealand and Australia were far away from kith and kin and the transportation costs were enormous. Canada seemed to be the only possible choice.[2]

When the choice had been made for Canada it became necessary to rationalize the decision. Perhaps for some the most important justification, and their strongest support, was their view of life. For the orthodox Calvinists their decision lay in God's hands. He who had predetermined each man's fate and existence before time itself would show the way. Earnest prayers not to go often went unanswered, seemingly indicating God's desire for them to pack up and leave. The assurance that a Calvinist church, the Christian Reformed Church, was prepared to aid them in their settlement and reestablish their church life in the New World gave comfort and promised at least an approximation of the society they knew at home.

The view of emigration as a calling from God imparted a holy gloss or rationalization over their more mundane needs and desires. The worldly needs and problems that had bedevilled them could be seen as a kind of testing. Sorrow at the loss of home and homeland were regarded as necessary burdens God imposed to work His will. That Canada offered economic and social opportunity was the reward for obedience. It was clear that they were not simply going to become rich, they had in fact much to teach the Canadians, both religiously and socially.

Unfortunately this self-assurance, shared by many non-Calvinist immigrants, this protection against the harsh reality of what they were doing, was often transformed into a kind of arrogance, which bred the idea that Canadians had done rather poorly with their birthright and talents. Some have said it was an arrogance that grew out of their fear of the unknown, a compensatory reaction that many immigrants manifest. It was a self-righteousness that led to exclusivity and a distinct distance between the first-generation immigrants and the Canadians. This attitude existed before they embarked on the ships, for they came not as refugees, effusively grateful for rescue, but as a tribe on the move, with suspicion and cold assessment in their eyes, getting the measure of their neighbours and expecting little but what they could provide for themselves.

HAMMERING OUT THE POLICY

The growing public interest in emigration also awakened the dormant emigration societies. In response to public and governmental pressure they began to reorganize and upgrade their staffs from the few faithful and true believers who had kept the idea of emigration alive during the bitter years. Private emigration organizations and individuals also mushroomed and the press was full of ideas, projections and plans, and rumours about the overseas possibilities. It happened so quickly that J.A. Hartland, the director of the Netherlands Emigration Foundation, began to worry that it might signal a return of the uncontrolled propagandizing of the twenties.[3] This was not to be the case.

The Dutch government did not shrink from what it regarded to be a national necessity. While it might have mixed feelings about encouraging part of its population to leave the country, it felt it had little choice. Emigration could simply not be allowed to progress in the laissez-faire manner it had in the past. Prospective emigrants not only had to be informed, processed, and transported, but all of this had to be done in a planned fashion. Private organizations could neither be expected nor allowed to take the burden on themselves. Failed emigrants could destroy future recruitment and the wrong kind of emigration could rob the Netherlands of an adequate supply of skilled industrial workers so necessary for future development. From 1945 onward the government was to take on more and more of the financing and organization of emigration and the old policy of benign disinterest was turned around to one of government control and direction.

To initiate this policy the government turned to the Netherlands Emigration Foundation. This organization had far-reaching contacts in the Netherlands and in potential countries of immigration. It had proved itself in the past to be financially disinterested in emigration and had sought simply to organize the movement for the maximum benefit of those who were leaving the Netherlands. In February of 1946, the government requested all overseas consuls and embassies as well as officials of the Ministry of Foreign Affairs to channel requests for immigrants and information on immigration to the NEF.[4]

Meanwhile, it had instructed its ambassadors in prospective countries to feel out their host country's attitudes toward Dutch immigration. The Dutch ambassador in Ottawa, J. Snouck Hurgronje, replied in January of 1946 that tentative talks with the Canadian government had been rather unproductive. There seemed to be an opportunity for at least 1,000 Dutch farmers but the demobilization of the Canadian military and the lack of available transport ruled out any immigration at the present. Immigration politics within the Canadian government were uncertain, and the Minister of Mines and Resources, whose department had responsibility for immigration, had replied to persistent requests from the Dutch ambassador that he was "not in state to decide on any long range immigration policy." As a result, the Dutch government received only meagre comfort from the fact that Canada's immigration policy permitted entry to wives and children of soldiers and highly trained and needed specialists. Any hopes of opening the doors to Canada were to be frustrated, at least for the moment.[5]

The Dutch government and the NEF did not give up completely. Many Canadian soldiers, now returned home, wrote to friends and relatives in Holland offering to intercede and find them work if they could get visas. They were joined by the old immigrants who were now Canadian citizens and were willing and able to sponsor new settlers.[6] The arrival in Canada of some 1,886 Dutch war brides and 428 children also helped to put pressure on the Canadian government to permit the entrance of their relatives.

Other factors carried greater weight. The Canadian government's experience with Dutch immigrants over the past fifty or more years had been generally positive. The Dutch had acquitted themselves well in Canada. Furthermore, Canada had need of farm labour and skilled labour and Hollanders made good workers. The Dutch immigrant was ambitious and within a few years generally attempted to become independent. From an economic standpoint, the admittance of this class of people had much to recommend it.

Of more immediate concern was the question of trade with the Netherlands. Obviously, the Netherlands, with its agricultural difficulties, would need to buy grains from overseas and Canada was interested in filling that need. It is unclear what direct and immediate impact this trade opportunity had on the Canadian immigration policy, but it is interesting to note that views of Dutch immigration, particularly in the Department of Mines and Resources, changed with the arrival of the Dutch agricultural attaché, A.S. Tuinman, in September of 1946. Tuinman had been instructed by the Dutch government to tie immigration and grain purchases together in one package and he was given complete charge of any future emigration to Canada.[7] It appears that the Canadian government found the arrangement a useful one and agreed to accept 500 unmarried Dutch farm workers in the spring of 1947. Because of need for agricultural labour in Canada, approximately 2,738 Dutch immigrants arrived in Canada in 1947, a far greater number than had been agreed upon in the first discussions.[8]

The Dutch government was not completely satisfied with the arrangements they had made with the Canadian government. Eventually, though, a flexible system was hammered out between the Dutch and Canadian governments that permitted the immigration of Dutch nationals according to the demands of the Canadian labour market. While the initial understanding was for the majority of immigrants to be agriculturalists, it was understood that as needs developed in the Canadian work force other occupations would be given greater priority.

Of prime concern, both to the Dutch and Canadian governments, was the question of how the immigration was to be regulated. Fortunately for the Canadian government, their part involved minimal expense with maximum profit. Recruitment in the Netherlands was to be left to the emigration societies. Limited selection and screening was done under the aegis of these societies, with the Netherlands Emigration Foundation keeping a watchful eye over quality and suitability. Canadian responsibility was limited to interviewing screened applicants and giving them a medical examination to see if they met Canadian standards. The NEF was also responsible for transportation from the Netherlands to Canada.

On arrival in Canada the immigrants were once again to be medically inspected and then handed over to Dutch-Canadian organizations for placement. The Canadian government demanded that every single immigrant or family head have a position before he embarked for Canada. The job of finding employment for the immigrants fell mainly to the NEF, the Dutch agricultural attaché in Ottawa, and representatives of Dutch-Canadian organizations. It was clear that Canada was interested in receiving Dutch immigrants but only if the situation was convenient, the problems minimal, and the benefits obvious.[9]

BUILDING THE MACHINERY

Canadians who came in contact with Dutch immigrants in the post-war period tended to regard them as they had other immigrating national groups: as a homogeneous entity. The pre-war Dutch immigrants had settled in and established a good reputation and few Canadians envisioned any serious problems in the integration of the new wave of immigrants. They were, however, unaware of the serious divisions that had, in some sense, separated and fractured the Dutch society and would be transplanted to Canada. Such divisions would work against the creation of a unified group consciousness and often presented Canadians with mystifying and unique problems.

Since the latter half of the nineteenth century Dutch society has been divided into a number of *zuilen* or pillars comprised of adherents of particular religious and ideological views. The three main pillars are composed of the Protestants, the Catholics, and the religiously non-aligned. The Protestant pillar is further divided into two subgroups, the Dutch Reformed and the Calvinists, the "one more liberal-minded and undogmatic, the other more aggressive dogmatic Calvinists."[10] For generations each group had created its own institutions and programs according to its beliefs. The result is an exclusiveness or separation between groups that has been referred to as religious-ideological segregation. This segregation cuts across class and economic barriers and creates a situation in which group members prefer to associate only with those who share their ideology. Therefore, each group has its own schools, political parties, press, television network, labour unions, emigration societies, and other organizations.

Such *zuil* or pillar orientation created confusion and problems in the area of emigration, resulting in an ongoing struggle between the secular and sectarian emigration societies as each sought to meet the perceived needs of its own groups. The great number of prospective emigrants, the limited amount of subsidy available, and the Dutch government's determination to make the movement work as well as possible, helped along by the Canadian government's express desire to work with only one central emigration organization, forced an accommodation between the various groups. By 1953, the Dutch government had placed emigration under one central control, the Emigration Commission. From this point on emigration from the Netherlands was more orderly and controlled.

In Canada, however, problems arose. The Canadian government had made its initial contacts with the Dutch agricultural attaché and assumed that his office would be largely responsible for co-ordinating and settling the new immigrants in Canada. It soon became obvious that the attaché did not have the funds or manpower to undertake such a project. While his office could serve a co-ordinating function between the Dutch and Canadian governments, he simply did not have the staff to scour the countryside looking for jobs for the potential immigrants. He had a few employees available to meet the boats and do the paperwork necessary in getting approved jobs and applications back to the Netherlands, but he was dependent on private citizens and organizations for the majority of placements.[11]

The placement system was essentially quite simple. The NEF (later the Netherlands Emigration Service) sent the names and files of suitable applicants to the Dutch agricultural attaché in Ottawa. His office sent these names and family descriptions to the Canadian superintendent of settlement, who passed them on to the district settlement officers, who in turn gave them to the Dutch-Canadian representatives who were to find suitable employment and accommodation. Given the small number of Dutch Canadians, the vast majority of jobs were provided by English Canadians. Once jobs were located the file had to be approved by representatives of the Immigration Service of the Department of Mines and Resources. These approvals were forwarded to the Canadian embassy and the NES. If the applicants were deemed medically fit they would be granted visas. The NES then booked transportation and forwarded the list of approved emigrants to the Dutch agricultural attaché in Ottawa and the Dutch-Canadian organizations. The Dutch-Canadian representatives in Canada were to make sure that the immigrant reached his destination after arrival in Canada.

The first private organization in the field prepared to help in the placement and settlement of Dutch immigrants was the Immigration Committee for Canada of the Christian Reformed Church. Beginning work as early as 1947, it was funded by the Christian Reformed Church in the United States and Canada. Its representatives and home missionaries sought to find jobs and help in the placement of rural Calvinists who were coming to Canada. Closely aligned with the Christian Emigration Central in the Netherlands, it was an aggressive and extraordinarily effective organization.

It was joined in the work by the Social Action Department of the Catholic Immigration Aid Society, which was in daily contact with diocesan directors of immigration in each of the sixty Canadian dioceses (1950). The Director of Immigration worked with clergy (sometimes Dutch) and lay people to find sponsors, jobs, and placements. The majority of the work was undertaken by Canadian parish priests who provided the spiritual, financial, and social aid so necessary for the new arrivals. It should be noted that the Catholic Church's organization was developed to aid all immigrants, not just the Dutch, although a number of priests, such as Fathers Ver Hagen (Alberta) and Van Wezel (Ontario), made an extraordinary impact on Dutch Catholic settlement.[12] Some 24 per cent of the total immigration was Roman Catholic even though Catholics made up 38 per cent of the total population of the Netherlands at the time.[13] They were proportionately less rural than the Calvinists and this was a rural emigration.

The third organization to help the settlement of Dutch immigrants was the Immigration Committee for Canada of the Reformed Church in America. Not in the field until 1950 due to the mistaken belief that Reformed immigrants would assimilate rapidly into Canadian society and church life, it was supported by the Reformed Church in America and had close ties to the Reformed Emigration Society in the Netherlands. Its funds were comparatively small and it had few agents.[14]

Thus, four separate entities – the agricultural attaché, the Catholics, the Christian Reformed, and the Reformed – were active in the immigration work. Non-denominational immigrants made up 7 per cent of the arrivals and were cared for by all groups, but especially by the agricultural attaché.[15] However, the division of responsibility was not all that clear, for the Christian Reformed organization quickly dominated the immigration work. With churches in Ontario, Alberta, and British Columbia, it had contacts in the most viable settlement areas. These churches quickly established local immigration committees that aided the fieldmen in finding jobs and homes. Aggressively evangelistic, some saw an opportunity to enlarge the Calvinist community by providing service to all immigrants of the Reformed tradition. As a result, immigrants who had belonged to the Reformed Church in the Netherlands were aided and encouraged to join the Christian Reformed fellowship. This led inevitably to charges from Reformed Church officials of "raiding" and questions by the Canadian government as to whether immigrants were being placed with a concern for their best economic futures.[16] Despite such criticism the Christian Reformed Church provided jobs, housing (some congregations had purchased houses especially designated for temporary shelter of immigrants), and some measure of post-arrival care.

The Canadian government quickly realized that Dutch immigration was not homogeneous. Religious differences appeared to create profound distance between the groups, making co-ordination of immigration more difficult and at times seriously hindering the settling in and success of the immigrants. While Canadian immigration officials held regular meetings with the various organizations and a general policy was achieved, there seemed to be continual friction between the various churches. This friction not only angered the Canadians but produced sniping and conflict that threatened the government's willingness to work with any or all of them. The agricultural attaché was attacked by the Christian Reformed as being motivated solely by economic desire, while he in turn attacked them as being hypocritical empire-builders tied by an unbending dogmatism. The Reformed resented the religious superiority complex of the Christian Reformed, who in turn accused them of abandoning Reformed and spiritual necessities. The Roman Catholics, dedicated to integration and assimilation, found the squabbles unnecessary and undignified.[17]

Out of this conflict grew an accommodation by which they could undertake what they had been set up to do – help the immigrant. This was eventually to produce the Canadian Netherlands Immigration Council in 1955. It was to be the co-ordinating body for all Christian immigration organizations in Canada, with its primary aim to promote the integration of Netherlands immigrants into Canadian life. Funding for CNIC was provided by the sponsoring churches; despite attempts to get subsidies from the Canadian and Dutch governments, such financial help was not forthcoming.[18]

One of the Council's continuing responsibilities was the Young Farmer's Program, which brought farmers' sons to Canada and placed them in temporary employment on Canadian farms, with the aim of introducing them to Canadian conditions and encouraging their emigration to Canada. The CNIC also sponsored lecture series in the Netherlands to stir emigration.[19] But the number and quality of immigrants seemed to decline rapidly after the mid-1950's as the Netherlands regained its economic footing and as personal income and social conditions improved. By 1962 the numbers had fallen from a high of 20,500 in 1953 to less than 2,000. One CNIC member sadly remarked, "As far as the quality is concerned, I must often admit, that like the milk in the Netherlands, the cream is gone."[20]

Nevertheless, from 1947 to 1970 almost 185,000 Dutch immigrants entered Canada. The religiously oriented immigration societies handled the bulk of that movement at a combined cost of over $2 million. In terms of service and aid, the per capita cost was extremely low, due in large measure to the sacrifice and unpaid labour of hundreds of interested people. Their imagination and expertise greatly aided the integration and settlement of thousands of immigrants and made the movement the success that it was. In response to need, they had buried their conflicting ideologies.

NOTES

1. Interview with A.S. Tuinman, October, 1978, Calgary, Alberta. One of the more active recruiters in Canada for Dutch labour was George Horlings of Holland Marsh.
2. Tuinman interview.
3. J.A. Hartland to A. Warnaar, 21 September 1945, NESC, GAI.
4. Tuinman interview.
5. J. Snouck Hurgronje to the Minister of External Affairs, 7 January 1946, NESC, GAI.
6. Ministry of Social Affairs to Ministry of External Affairs, March, 1946, NESC, GAI.
7. Tuinman interview.
8. Oosterman, *To Find a Better Life*, p. 92.
9. Tuinman interview.
10. J.P. Kruijt, "The Influence of denominationalism in social life and organized patterns," in K. McRae, ed., *Consociational Democracy: Political Accommodation in Segmented Societies* (1974), p. 130.
11. Tuinman interview.
12. Mrs. Ann Felix to author, 6 March 1980.
13. Oosterman, *To Find a Better Life*, p. 94.
14. For an early report on the activities of this organization, see *The Canadian*

Work of the Reformed Church of America, 9 October 1952, in the John Heersink Papers, author's possession.

15. Oosterman, *To Find a Better Life*, p. 94.
16. A.S. Tuinman to N.E.F., 4 January 1949, NESC, GAI.
17. A.S. Tuinman to N.E.F., 2 November 1948; T. Cnossen to N.E.F., 14 December 1948, NESC, GAI.
18. Minutes of Canadian Netherlands Immigration Council Meeting, 3 July 1956, Burlington, John Heersink Papers.
19. Confidential Report on October, 1959, trip to Holland, January, 1960, John Heersink papers.
20. T. Polet to J. Heersink, 28 December 1956, John Heersink Papers.

SIX

On to Canada!

THE JOURNEY

The great wave of emigration enthusiasm generated by governments, organizations, friends, and even potential emigrants themselves did little to prepare the emigrants for the hard decisions and problems that arose when commitment had to replace discussion. These difficulties were compounded by the fact that families now began to outnumber the single men and women who had made up much of the emigration movement prior to the Second World War. Most emigrating families were to learn, much to their dismay, that actually leaving the Netherlands often presented as many difficulties as settling in Canada.

One of the most difficult problems families had to face was internal disunity if not all members agreed that emigration was either necessary or justified. Sometimes the parents became immovable; sometimes a single member of the family, such as a mother or a daughter, refused to go. Threats of abandonment generally worked, although one doubts how serious the threat was. In most cases strong family ties and discipline held them together as a unit. This meant sacrifice, something most often made by the women. Mothers feared the loss of married family and relatives and the tight, sheltered life of the Dutch countryside. To them the dangers of Canadian life seemed greater than the rewards. Perhaps they also realized that, even more than the menfolk, they would be strangers in Canada. Young women who were engaged or had serious love interests were pulled between family and fiancés and were forced to choose. Authoritarian controls often brought about the obedience of the wives in a grudging fashion, while daughters either went unwillingly, got married as soon as possible, or convinced their fiancés to go along. In any case, the decision to go sometimes led to conflict and tearful interludes.

Even if all were agreed, there were other problems. Young men liable for the military draft had to request exemption and while this was practically a foregone conclusion, particularly if they were accompanying family, there were anxious moments.[1] There was also the question of subsidization of expenses. Starting in 1948 the Dutch government, believing that the agricultural crisis would inevitably force out surplus workers, provided only minimal financial support for transportation to those families who had inadequate funds for the journey overseas. Unfortunately, those on the borderline of eligibility often found it necessary to commit all their savings, which meant they arrived in Canada with empty pockets. Even those with cash reserves or property in the Netherlands found that because of monetary restrictions they were limited in the amount of money they could take along. Because of Holland's critical economic situation persons over the age of fifteen were allowed only $100 apiece and those under fifteen only $50.[2] The remainder of their funds was to remain in the Netherlands as either real property or bank deposits. As economic conditions bettered in the 1950's access to these reserves was opened up to the emigrants.

Perhaps the greatest difficulty, and the one that generated the most fear in families, was the possibility of medical rejection.[3] It was difficult enough to leave a son or daughter behind who had chosen to stay, but what was one to do if a family member was rejected for a physical or mental problem? How could a family abandon an even slightly retarded child, a son with a spot on his lung, a daughter with a crooked limb, or even a parent with a heart or kidney condition? All the assurances that such a person would never become a public liability in Canada met with sympathetic but unchanging rejection on the part of the Canadian doctors. While an occasional appeal to a higher authority in London was sometimes successful, the majority of such families saw their dreams come to a bitter end and were forced to surrender their emigration plans. Such rejections sometimes led to the emigration of those single members of the family who were acceptable, which meant the break-up of families.[4]

Even if the family passed the inspection, a number of hurdles still had to be overcome. They were inevitably faced with a barrage of advice from friends, relatives, neighbours, and even the public press. Just about everyone had heard horror stories from previous emigrants about the difficulty of life in Canada. Inadequate housing, cruel and unfeeling employers, and the lack of social services were stressed as dangers to the emigrants. Some emphasized the hard life, insecurity, and loneliness they would have to face. Wasn't it better to abandon that foolish dream now before the fatal step had been taken? How would it feel to come back disgraced and beaten, having to ask for charity?[5]

Others simply stoked the fires of enthusiasm, urged their neighbours and friends on, and promised that they, too, would soon join the thousands going to Canada. The public press, religious weeklies, and farmers' magazines sometimes painted a demi-paradise. It is true that they emphasized the necessity of hard work and perseverance, but what person so far committed did not believe he had the capabilities? Religious emigration societies seemed to promise the heavens.[6] It was like a giant carnival, with the bewildered future emigrants standing in the middle, unsure as to the direction they ought to take. If anything, many went simply to end the argument, the caterwauling, the bickering, and the pain of indecision.

Now there was no turning back. Now they could only go ahead, and that meant selling out and getting rid of what they could not take along, which seemed to be most of what they possessed. First of all the suitcases had to be packed with clothes for the trip and the immediate period after arrival. Linens, bedclothes, and sometimes even a pot or two were tucked away. Heavy underclothes, woollen undershirts, topcoats, and woollen caps were packed in expectation of the cooler northern temperatures. Soon there was no more room and the remainder was set aside to go in the huge packing crate. Yet they were permitted only 2,500 pounds, and all too soon the chairs and tables, dishes, and the whole array of household goods took up all the available room. Grandmother's dishes, the picture of the farm, the Turkish rug for the table had to be taken along, but there was always so much left. Poor or well-to-do, the emigrants could never take everything they wanted to and they were forced to dispose of the rest. Most families held auction sales, but they were in competition with those of hundreds of others who were also planning to leave. Often the results were disappointing and the purse remained critically thin.[7]

Then one day everything had been done. The wooden crate of possessions that had stood in the yard had been forwarded to the ship; the farm had been sold or rented to someone else; and the stuffed suitcases stood waiting among the few remaining beds in the otherwise empty rooms. The ship's passage had been paid to Halifax or Quebec; vouchers or tickets guaranteed the rail trip to places they had never heard of - Belleville, Hamilton, Winnipeg, Lethbridge: the words rolled strangely on the tongue. The night before departure Mother had sewn a few precious Canadian dollars inside Father's coat, to get around the monetary restrictions. All that was left was the leavetaking, saying good-bye to parents or relatives, strong faces filled with suppressed tears, some of which could not be withheld. Firm handshakes, the rush to the taxi or bus and then to the train, and suddenly all the enthusiasm tasted bitter as the realization dawned that it might be good-bye forever.

By the time the train reached Rotterdam, emotions were once again under control. Parents had come to some kind of fatalistic acceptance of their future. The past was yet very real to them; the close-knit village and church life, their friends and relatives, all crowded their thoughts. The children were already savouring the sense of adventure. Suitcases were wrestled from the train and out to the quay they went, waiting for the first sight of the ship, their ship, the one that would carry them to Canada.

For some, that first glimpse of their ship must have been disappointing. They knew that the Netherlands had few passenger ships available for emigration, for those not captured by the Germans had been converted into allied troopships. In response to the growing crush of emigration the Dutch government diverted a number of troopships for this purpose. What had been sufficient in an emergency for soldiers and evacuees hardly satisfied the needs of the departing emigrants.

One of the first shocks to the emigrant's already depleted store of confidence was the separation of family members; the men and boys over twelve were assigned to a different section of the ship. Expecting perhaps comfortable accommodation with his wife and family in their own stateroom, the emigrant found himself with hundreds of men and boys in large rooms filled with canvas hammocks strung between pipe frames. The conditions for women and children were similar.

Modesty and privacy were practically impossible under such conditions and only a draped blanket preserved even a shred of one's own territory. Showers and toilet facilities were built for efficiency and cleanliness, not privacy, and with the exception of drinking water, all other needs had to be met with seawater. Meals were served cafeteria style, in shifts, and eaten at long tables on aluminum mess trays. Sitting down as a family was an impossibility, as was keeping the strawberry jam out of the mashed turnips and potatoes. While food was plentiful, it was tasteless in an institutional fashion, but for many this was to mean little, as the ship began wallowing its way across the ocean.

Those lucky enough to have fine weather on their passage spent most of the time on the limited space on deck. Even in bad weather people fled from nauseating odours that began seething through the ship. Hot days intensified the problem and emphasized the inadequate ventilation. Stormy days cut off the circulation of air and produced an overwhelming closeness.

Crying children and moaning seasick passengers meant that peace and quiet simply did not exist. Tempers frayed and conflict between parents and children and neighbours became a common occurrence. The occasional visit of a minister or priest who might be accompanying the group, or a Sunday religious service, was a welcome respite. To the many who made their way to Canada in those ships it was an unforgettable experience, one to be taken out and discussed in later years, an event that even became a badge of courage when compared with the experiences of their fellow immigrants who were fortunate enough to have come over on regular passenger liners or even on airplanes. It became a sign of toughness, an initiation into the hardships of their life in Canada.[8]

The trip across the ocean, even in the troopships, had its positive side. Men and women from different towns and villages became acquainted with each other for the first time. Provincial and parochial ideas and attitudes began to undergo a subtle change. The old rivalries between Zeelanders and Friesians or Groningers and Hollanders seemed less important now that they were all emigrants with the same hopes and fears. They shared different pasts but only one common future, and many began to realize that they would have to work together in the future to survive. Perhaps for the first time many put aside the prejudices and suspicions they had held of people from other areas.

With the young, the prejudices seemed to be less deeply imbedded and they quickly explored the ship making the acquaintance of other youthful emigrants, making plans together for the future. Get-togethers, singing, games, and other organized group activities would be more common on the later, more luxurious passenger liners, but even on the troopships there was always someplace to talk and share ideas. Some even managed to strike up friendships that led to stolen moments of endearment, and the age-old search for a mate continued unimpeded by bad weather or a lack of privacy.

And yet, despite the camaraderie and changing attitudes, some old prejudices remained. The distance between Catholic and Protestant, so noticeable in rural areas, continued to hold sway. While the narrow suspicions might be somewhat diminished, there remained a deep chasm between the two religious groups. It seemed clear that in Canada, as in Holland, the Calvinists would go in a different direction from their Catholic countrymen.

As the ships neared the coast of Canada a sense of expectation grew among the passengers. Seasickness and the crowded conditions, the everlasting noise of the children, all faded away before a growing excitement. Those whose ships went up the St. Lawrence to Quebec City or Montreal marvelled at the green farms and white houses stretching away from the shoreline. Others arriving in Saint John or Halifax were struck by the bleakness and even apparent poverty of those port cities.[9]

The first views of the new land elicited mixed emotions; the green, tree-lined shores of Canada were nothing like home. The questions and fears, which had been temporarily put away on the journey, quickly reappeared as the landing became imminent. What exactly would await them? What was their employer like? Where would they settle?

Long discussions with other immigrants seldom led to any hard and fast conclusions. Stories about the success of their relatives or friends seemed to bear little relevance to their own situations. Occasionally there was someone on board who had already gone through the process and had returned to the Netherlands only to emigrate again when conditions changed. Usually they were only familiar with the areas they had previously settled in and seldom knew the answers to questions about London, Niagara Falls, or Lacombe. Even the assurances of accompanying Netherlands emigration officials or representatives of the various church groups involved in settlement in Canada seemed inadequate to dispel the feeling that it had all been some awful mistake.

Near the shore the pilot boat with the fieldman and government officials came alongside. Customs and immigration documents were checked. Transportation was laid out and instructions were given as to train departures, transfers, and the stops where friends, relatives, or responsible agents would meet them and take them to their destinations.

Somehow, the disembarkation was made. Once in a while they were met by Canadian and Dutch government officials who gave them a welcome reception in the names of their respective governments and promised a healthy and wealthy future. Much of this was to be remembered as a blur of action and noise, highlighted by a last view of the homeland's flag whipping in the wind on the stern of the ship as the national anthem played on the ship's loudspeaker system. Then on they went, through customs and immigration, into lines and onto the trains.[10]

For some there was a little time before the trains left and they took advantage of it to explore their new land. The buildings at dockside Halifax or Quebec City or even Montreal were unimpressive, wooden, ramshackle. They lined dusty streets leading into the strange cities. Some found the small corner store with its all but inexhaustible supply of oranges, bananas, and ice cream – delicacies still either rare or expensive in the Netherlands. The carefully hoarded dollars were taken out and a few spent for a treat, then back to the train and the journey into the heart of Canada.

The Canadian railways, just beginning to readjust their networks from the necessities of wartime and unprepared for the new rush of immigrants, found themselves forced to put all available cars on the tracks. Colonists' cars, which had done duty since the first decades of the century, were rushed back into service. The immigrants found that windows would either not close or not open, that seats were hard, drinking water was often scarce, at least cool water, and that everything, including themselves, quickly became covered by a thin layer of soot from the belching steam engines.

The trains puffed on day and night, stopping and starting, delivering passengers to their destinations. Fieldmen often rode along, sharing the accommodation, answering interminable questions, and making sure that the immigrants detrained at the correct places or made the proper connections. Peering through grimy windows these new immigrants were dismayed, as those who had preceded them in the last fifty years had been, by the virtual emptiness of the land. The vast distances, the interminable trees, and the apparently dilapidated condition of the farms that could be seen from the train struck an unhappy and discordant note. The relatively settled areas of Quebec were quickly swallowed up, to be followed by the settled farms of Ontario and the expansive landscape of the Prairies.

At last they arrived at their destination. They detrained hoping to be met by either church officials or family, someone who spoke Dutch. Sometimes only the farmer was there. Baggage was rescued and packed away, and it was off to a new beginning. Some found to their chagrin that the farmer or employer who had sponsored them had changed his mind and a further journey was necessary to another employer. The ever-concerned fieldman worked miracles and within a short time the problems had been solved. Immigrants were introduced to farmers and the waiting lines were finally dispersed.

Most immigrants had little idea of the tremendous amount of work that had been done simply to get them from Holland to Canada, but they did understand that the fieldmen who were to help them at their arrival symbolized the very best of that effort. It was these men who had received their applications and found them jobs. Most of them had been born in the Netherlands and had emigrated to Canada prior to the Second World War. They not only spoke English and Dutch, but had an easy familiarity with the employers and conditions in their own areas. Working with the missionaries, the church organizations, the government employment bureaus, the railways, and anyone else who expressed an interest in immigration, they attempted to ease the transition from one country to another. Often home missionaries such as Rev. P.W. Hoekstra of Lethbridge, Alberta, or John Gritter of Hamilton, Ontario, served as fieldmen in addition to their tasks of caring for the spiritual needs of their congregations.

The fieldmen gave service far beyond the requirements of duty. Inadequately recompensed, they often sacrificed health, family, and personal business to serve the needs of the bewildered immigrants. One fieldman vividly recalled the time when he had immigrants in his attic, bedroom, and basement and had others waiting at the train station for placement.[11] The motivations of these men differed as greatly as the men themselves. Some saw their work as a simple response to human need, others as an extension of their personal faith; a very few regarded it as a means of building congregations and extending the work of their particular church. Most, while sharing some of these ideas, simply remembered the difficulties they or their parents had had in adjusting to the new society and set out to ameliorate the worst of these difficulties as best they could. They were practical, knowledgeable, energetic, and, perhaps most of all, optimistic, both about Canada and about the possibility of success for the immigrants. This optimism remained the dominant theme in their work with their newly arrived countrymen.

FINDING WORK

The immigrants who left the train station with friends and relatives were spared the unnerving experience of immediately having to meet their new boss. Introduced by the fieldman, the employer tried to talk to his new employees in English, most often getting no greater response than an inappropriate "yes" or an uncomprehending shrug. Despite entreaty and warning, few immigrants had bothered to learn English. If the boss spoke a little German or even occasionally French some contact could be made. Those immigrants who went to relatives or Dutch-Canadian farmers were exceptionally lucky, as the method of communication in other cases, at least until some skill in the English language had been acquired, was by sign language and a kind of pidgin English. Children who had taken a few years of English instruction in school sometimes served as interpreters for their parents, although their ability was often minimal. The ride to the farm was usually a silent one, pregnant with apprehension on the part of both nationalities.

There it was, the new home! What was it, what had it been? A chicken barn quickly converted for human habitation? A log cabin having done service to generations of farm families? A horse barn, uninsulated, with one stove for cooking and heating, with pipes meandering from room to room? A good brick house set pleasantly among the trees with yard and garden? A migrant worker's shack infested with mice with one window and a beaten mud yard? A plain wooden house, empty and yawning, far from neighbours and town, without a speck of furniture? It conjured up nothing familiar; it was just a building filled with loneliness. The greater the disappointment, the greater the sense of loss. Men and women stoically set their faces, but the tears would come. Beds were made, sheets and blankets unpacked, the faces scrubbed, and dinner attempted. Their own possessions were still packed away in the "box" either still at sea or on the train or shunted into some freight yard far from their destination. They were denied even the familiarity of their possessions.

Those first few weeks of adjusting to a new environment, different in every way from that which they had known, tapped the reserves of strength of all members of the family. The father was immediately cast into the world of work, ploughing, using machinery, planting or thinning beets, or working in the orchards. Even though the work may have been similar to that done in the Netherlands, styles of working were often different, and most difficult of all was understanding the boss. Often work had to be demonstrated and frustration on the part of the employer and his new helper was common. At least the husband was occupied, and if he had sons who could find work on the farm he had company. Sometimes the sons sought work with local farmers or employment in neighbouring towns or cities. The necessity to supplement the family income made plans for returning to school a practical impossibility for those able to work. The family became a unit of survival, drawn together by circumstances if not by choice.

The wife generally found the adjustment to the new life extremely difficult. Women who had lived on farms or in small villages or towns, close to friends and family and with ready access to bakers, butchers, and other services, found themselves isolated in rural Ontario or on the southern Alberta prairie. With the younger children at school and the other family members working in the field, there was plenty of time for thinking and for the pangs of fear and loneliness. Cleaning, baking, and mending, no matter how energetically done, never seemed to fill the empty hours. While many husbands were not unsympathetic and some helped in the home to lift the burden, they smothered their apprehension and fear and maintained an optimistic and hopeful outlook, refusing to surrender to depression.[12]

The children made the transition more easily. Most of those who went to school found that, while language skills were definitely a problem, education in the Netherlands appeared to have been superior to that in Canada. Spending an obligatory period in the lower grades was expected, but within six or twelve months they had generally been moved up to or ahead of their old-country grade level. Teachers found the majority of immigrant children to be hard-working, well behaved, and quick to catch on and rewarded their efforts with rapid advancement. Although there were occasional cries of "D.P. [displaced person] go home," Dutch children were relatively well accepted by their peers, no doubt a reflection of the general Canadian attitude that the Dutch were excellent immigrants. Language skills were quickly mastered on the playground and in school and within a few months the immigrant children were fluently bilingual, often to the consternation of the parents, who found it difficult to accept the changes the children were undergoing. Those who could accept the changes found the children an invaluable help in talking to the boss, buying groceries, or slowly learning the language.

It soon became evident that practically every member of the family had to be committed to the economic maintenance of the unit. Older children accepted the inevitability of work rather than school as soon as they were fourteen. Daughters as well as sons worked on the farms, often alongside their mothers, who had never worked outside the home in the Netherlands except perhaps to help with the chores in and around the barns. Where possible, positions as domestics or factory workers were found for the older girls and boys in neighbouring towns or cities, while young children had their own farm chores. The pooling of labour inevitably led to the pooling of finances, usually controlled by the father. The children were given pocket money and the remainder of their wages was put into a "kitty" that would eventually buy the family's independence.[13]

While over half of the immigrants prior to 1950 went to farms, an increasing number found employment in the industrial, construction, and service areas of the Canadian work force. The Canadian government, responding to increased needs in this area, widened the door to those immigrants who were willing to work in the mines, bush camps, and isolated industries where more workers were required. Much of this immigration was made up of single men for whom accommodation was relatively easy to acquire. Camp barracks or boarding houses meant shared accommodation and relatively easy placement compared to the difficulty of finding room for immigrant families in already over-crowded cities.

These non-agricultural immigrants found their adjustment as traumatic as that of their farm counterparts. While many were not burdened by family, they also lacked the support of close relatives. Often geographically isolated from other Dutch immigrants, socially alienated because of language and customs, they were forced to adapt rapidly. Others living in urban areas, although less isolated from a Dutch community, felt lonely and often unhappy living on their own. In some cases single men boarded together, if possible with a Dutch family, in order to recreate a semblance of their past lives. The growing Dutch concentration in urban areas proved a magnet to the other immigrants who had found themselves isolated in the work camps and construction projects and they began to look for new jobs in those centres.

The non-agricultural immigrant, whether single or married, shared most of the same values with his farm counterpart. A good job, a decent place to live, and the opportunity to accumulate a stake for the future were also his priorities. To that end he looked to the Dutch community to provide a semblance of stability and continuity to help him integrate into the Canadian society.

NOTES

1. N.E.F. to Ministry of War, 12 August 1948, NESC, GAI.
2. N.E.F. to A.S. Tuinman, 8 March 1948, NESC, GAI.
3. N.E.F. List of Appeals to Chief Canadian Medical Officer, London,

12 January 1948, NESC, GAI. This list is particularly interesting because all the non-agricultural immigrants were turned down.

4. N.E.F. to A.S. Tuinman, 16 December 1948, NESC, GAI. This letter comments on some of the problems slowing down the emigration and remarks: "For many people emigration is an intoxication and therefore has to be completed as quickly as possible. If many months pass one has too much time to weigh the risks of emigration and one comes to the conclusion not to do it."

5. N.E.F. to A.S. Tuinman, 18 October 1948, NESC, GAI.

6. A.S. Tuinman to N.E.F., 2 November 1948, NESC, GAI.

7. A.S. Tuinman to N.E.F., 25 April 1949; N.E.F. to A.S. Tuinman, 8 March 1948, NESC, GAI.

8. Co-ordination of emigrants and transportation was always a serious problem for the Dutch government, the NEF, and the private organizations. Often ships were ready and emigrants were not, or vice versa. Tuinman interview.

9. Vis, "Report." The material concerning the Atlantic passage comes from immigrant interviews, newspaper and official reports, and personal experience. The clarity with which this journey is remembered establishes it as an event of deep significance.

10. A.S. Tuinman to N.E.F., 5 July 1947, NESC, GAI.

11. Interview with Bernard Nieboer, July, 1976, Iron Springs, Alberta.

12. Vis, Trip Impressions of Canada, October, 1947, NESC, GAI.

13. The material concerning arrival and early adjustment is derived from extensive immigrant interviews and interviews with fieldmen such as B. Nieboer and Fr. F. Ver Hagen and with government officials such as A.S. Tuinman and G. Stallinga.

SEVEN

Problems of Adjustment

THE NEW CHURCH

The initial difficulties the immigrants experienced in adjusting to the new environment were greatly lessened by the interest some Canadian and American churches showed in helping them settle in. While the mainline Canadian Protestant churches expressed little interest in the Dutch settlers, the Roman Catholics and particularly the Christian Reformed Church made significant efforts to aid them. As the majority of immigrants in this early post-war period were from a Calvinist background, their care became an increasing concern of the Christian Reformed Church.

The establishment of Christian Reformed mission stations and churches in Canada had been dealt a severe blow in the 1930's. The cut-off of immigration, the hard times, and the uncontrolled dispersal of families and single men searching for some kind of economic stability had weakened the existing church organizations. Mission work had been maintained, however, and where a ministerial appointment was not possible, elders continued the practice of holding services and reading prepared sermons. By the end of the war strong congregations, although not great in number, were looking forward to the resumption of immigration. Church organizations in Hamilton, Toronto, Holland Marsh, and the Windsor area of Ontario, as well as western congregations in Winnipeg, southern Alberta, Lacombe, Neerlandia, Edmonton, and Vancouver, were prepared to give aid and extend a welcome to new immigrants. These keystones would prove to be a tremendous benefit to both immigration organizations and to the immigrants themselves. Members of these congregations not only opened up their homes, found jobs, and gave advice, but they were active in the recruitment of immigrants for their particular areas.[1]

Some Christian Reformed farmers who had difficulty in finding farm help, particularly in the Holland Marsh, started contacting the Dutch embassy in Ottawa and making representations through the local federal MP to open up the immigration gates to their distressed cousins at home. When immigration finally became possible, such farmers began to acquire a significant work force of imported labour, usually relatives or friends, and they became important way-stations in the movement of immigrants from Holland to Canada.[2]

Concentration of immigrants in certain areas made possible the future organization of a church that could help retain the religious character of the immigrants. Although some fieldmen were reluctant to venture far from the environs of the church and perhaps occasionally overstocked an area beyond its supportive capacity, most regarded economic viability as the priority because they believed that, once financial security was established, a church was sure to follow in areas of concentration. Although this did bring them into occasional conflict with church authorities and led to some criticism that money was more important than faith to them, they persisted in their policy.[3] Charges against the fieldmen from the immigrants and the Canadian and Dutch governments of "congregation-building" at the cost of the immigrant were not easy to justify. All in all, the fieldmen and their organization struggled manfully to give the immigrants the best chance possible.

Once placement had been completed the difficult task of forming a church community among the Dutch Protestants was begun. Since the fieldman had lists of all the immigrants of his particular denomination, these were passed on to the ministers, missionaries, or church organizations. Almost immediately immigrants began meeting together, usually through a contact person, for the purpose of forming some kind of church community and holding services. Since the Christian Reformed Church is congregational in nature, elders and deacons were chosen by public vote and meetings quickly produced congregations. Money was collected for rental of church halls or basements, masonic halls, library rooms, or other facilities that would accommodate a gathering of people. Where churches or mission stations had already been formed in the past, this task was, of course, significantly easier. Out of meagre earnings and skimpy savings came offerings to get the church established.[4]

After a meeting place had been found, the problem of transport arose. Those with amenable employers got a ride or the loan of a truck as soon as a driver's licence was procured. Those who had cars or trucks gave lifts to as many as possible, some even building enclosed boxes, complete with stoves and benches, on the backs of the trucks. Some were forced to hitchhike while others took whatever public transportation was available. Like all immigrants, the Dutch quickly learned that in Canada a car was a necessity. It became the first important purchase used almost entirely for church attendance and grocery shopping. While transportation within the community was often primitive, the solidarity and personal goodwill generated by sharing rides to church are impossible to measure.

Provincial differences, regional dialects, and parochial suspicions were soon put aside. They were all immigrants facing the same problems, and they had to do the best they could under the circumstances. Friesians, Zeelanders, Groningers, and Hollanders sat down together, visited after the service, and

85

compared their problems and offered possible solutions. Sometimes, if the distances were great, lunches were brought so that a second service could be held in the afternoon without necessitating further travel. Friendships were formed, long afternoon visits with return transportation were arranged, discussions were initiated about conditions back in Holland and in Canada, and a sense of community was re-established.[5]

The Roman Catholic Church, with a limited number of Dutch-speaking priests, attempted to serve as many of its communicants as possible. Since the mass was in Latin, even the Dutch parishioners could feel at home in the fulfilment of their religious duties. Many Dutch Catholics, however, did have a problem with a confessional carried out in a foreign tongue. Some enterprising English-speaking priests used numbered "sin sheets" printed in Dutch, which only required pointing to specific numbers in order to begin the process of absolution and the preparation for the eucharist. Dutch immigrants were welcomed into the church and the Catholic community and they made rapid contact with their English-speaking neighbours. Minimal language skills were often more quickly achieved by them than by their fellow Protestant immigrants who continued the old-country language in their churches.[6]

The adherents of the state church of the Netherlands, the Hervormde Kerk (the Reformed Church), found themselves in a quandary. Prior to the early 1950's they had been encouraged by their home churches to align themselves with Canadian mainline churches such as the Presbyterian Church and United Church of Canada, but many Reformed immigrants found such advice unacceptable.

Language proved an almost insurmountable obstacle to integration in the new church communities. The immigrants understood little or nothing about what was going on in their adopted congregations. They missed the sense of community, welcome, and similarity in background they had had at home. Some drifted to the Christian Reformed Church (where some felt they were treated as "not quite religious enough second-class Christians") while others left the church completely or wrote complaining letters home about their abandonment in the religious wilderness of Canada. A number felt that the United Church, although recommended at home, had surrendered to the onslaught of liberal theology and bore little relationship to the "reformed" teachings that were part of their own religious heritage. As a result, study trips were undertaken by various Dutch officials and the Reformed Church of America was approached to enter the mission field in a manner similar to that of the Christian Reformed Church. Realizing the need, and willing to extend financial support for missionaries and fieldmen, the Reformed Church of America began organizing to serve the Reformed immigrants.[7]

It was clear that Dutch Protestant immigrants desired to retain their religious heritage in their new land. The development and growth of Canadian branches of the American Reformed and Christian Reformed churches of the United States made this possible. Without the American concern, financial support, and staffing of missionaries and ministers, the Dutch Protestants in

Canada would have had an extremely difficult time maintaining their traditional beliefs. In fact, the fear of religious dispersion and the slow death of Dutch Calvinism in Canada was one of the chief motivating forces for the American effort. The churches' concern for the physical, economic, and spiritual welfare of the immigrants also played a large part in the extension of aid.

Slowly but surely, a new community began to form, its interests dominated by conditions in Canada, its concerns centring on survival and the achievement of success. The church, whether Protestant or Catholic, became a meeting place for the immigrants and held them together in a unity of concern and shared problems.

THE NEW JOB

As Canada's industrialization and urbanization continued in the post-war period the Canadian government found itself faced with the spectre of rural depopulation. Demobilized soldiers with new skills, desires, and experiences were reluctant to return to the seemingly unrewarding life on the farm. As they found places for themselves in the cities the problems of agricultural production grew more pressing. This loss of labour threatened a significant decline in a sector of the economy essential to the survival of the nation. The importation of agricultural labour, it was hoped, would not only put an end to temporary labour shortages of workers but would establish a permanent agricultural base.[8]

Due to the nature of the placement system and the religious affiliation of the majority of the new Dutch immigrants, much of the settlement was initially concentrated in those provinces that had seen previous Dutch immigration. Southern and southwestern Ontario and southern and central Alberta attracted the majority of the immigrants, while southern British Columbia was not far behind. This solved such immediate problems as providing workers for the fruit orchards of the Niagara Peninsula and for the beet and tobacco fields of southwestern Ontario, replacing Japanese beet workers in southern Alberta, and placing dairy workers in Ontario, Alberta, and British Columbia. However, the fruit growing and dairy areas of Nova Scotia and the mixed farming districts of New Brunswick and the Eastern Townships of Quebec needed more labour, as did the farming areas of eastern and northern Ontario. In fact, most provinces became increasingly dependent on imported immigrant labour to meet their needs.

As the available jobs and settlement opportunities were taken up in the initial placement areas, the immigration organizations and the immigrants themselves began to take notice of possibilities elsewhere. New settlements were begun around Kentville, Nova Scotia, Fredericton, New Brunswick, Richmond, Quebec, Ottawa, Ontario, Brandon, Manitoba, Barrhead, Rocky Mountain House, Peers, and High River in Alberta, Smithers and Port Alberni in British Columbia, and in many other places.

No matter what the job, life seemed more difficult in Canada. Only a bare existence could be maintained on a married man's salary of $75 a month or a single man's $45 and room and board, even if the one-year contract stipulated free firewood, vegetables, milk, and accommodation for some lucky immigrants.[9] Other costs seemed to drain away what little money could be put aside. Protection against sickness and unemployment had been taken for granted in the Netherlands; in Canada, the immigrants were on their own. It was necessary to buy insurance against drug costs and a visit to the doctor or a stay in the hospital. Clothes that had been appropriate in the Netherlands, such as flannel or knitted woollen undershirts, were simply too hot for the Canadian climate. Wooden shoes, excellent for working on the land, quickly wore out and had to be replaced by leather or rubber ones. Canadian goods seemed less durable than Dutch ones and comparison between life in the Netherlands and that in Canada inevitably led to dissatisfaction and frustration.

The work itself often bore little relationship to the tasks they were familiar with. Thinning and hoeing beets, the similarly back-breaking labour of suckering tobacco plants or the endless stoop labour of picking tomatoes and stones, seldom resembled the farm tasks at home. Men who had always ploughed deep in the Dutch soil found such practices unacceptable in the dry-land farming areas of the Prairies, little knowing it destroyed the already scant moisture. Such simple things as the Canadians' failure to use manure, because of a wartime shortage of farm labour and the physical limits of an aging farm population, created misunderstandings and an unfavourable assessment of Canadian agricultural methods. Accustomed to intensive farming, the Dutch immigrants regarded every forkful of manure as a valuable commodity and were bewildered by the huge piles dominating some Ontario farmyards, unused, while the fields desperately needed fertilizer. Some Canadian farmers' casual treatment of farm equipment, often leaving it standing in the field exposed to the wind, rain, snow, and rust, was inexplicable to the immigrant who routinely had oiled and sharpened his spade before he put it away.

The Canadians' seemingly lackadaisical attitude and indifference to farming were confusing and irritating. The unpainted houses and ramshackle outbuildings, no doubt the victims of depression austerity, challenged the Dutch farm hand's traditional sense of order and neatness. Many began not only to desire to change things to what they had had in the old country but to believe that they could farm more successfully and profitably than the Canadians. It was not just a matter of security or success, but a matter of pride; the immigrant came to believe that he was a better farmer than his employer.[10]

The first wave of agricultural immigrants quickly began to live up to the hopes that both the Dutch and Canadian immigration officials had placed in them. Fearful that Canadians would respond unfavourably to competing hordes of foreign urban workers, both governments emphasized the temporary character of the Dutch immigrant's position as a farm labourer. They said that the movement was necessitated by critical agricultural problems in Holland and that these immigrants, "settlers" rather, were coming to Canada to labour temporarily in the agricultural sector and as quickly as possible begin farming on their own. Farm ownership and absorption into the Canadian agricultural sector as producers were the ultimate goals, not competition with Canadian workers.[11] Whether for propaganda purposes or not, the aim of the movement began to be realized for some immigrants within two or three years of their arrival in Canada.

By working on shares, renting land, or even purchasing farms, immigrants began to establish themselves. Families with older children became the first pioneers in this field. Father and mother and children pooled their incomes and labour and in this way acquired capital. The beginning years had established a knowledge of Canadian farming methods, purchasing, and marketing, which helped them in achieving independence. Fieldmen, missionaries, older settled immigrants, and helpful Canadians aided immigrants in the difficult process of striking out on their own. Deeds and the legal technicalities of land transfer, rentals, and share agreements were mastered. Crops were planted and harvested, and, despite shortfalls and occasional bad luck, the general movement was forward. The intensive farming experience of the immigrants stood them in good stead, particularly in the mixed farming areas of Ontario, Quebec, and the Maritimes. They adapted themselves to the prairie style of farming in sugar beets, grain, or cattle. Others turned to fruit farming or vegetable growing and displayed the energy and determination to succeed at any cost.[12]

Yet some did not succeed. For them the cost was too high. The unending labour was often impossibly demanding. The margin between success and failure was usually many extra hours in the fields. Skimping on food to pay other bills inevitably led to physical decline. The worries over payments, broken machinery, and the always capricious weather taxed the psychological strength of many who were already numbed by the strangeness of their alien environment. Even the support of friends and church and helpful neighbours could not stave off the feeling that nothing would succeed in this new land.

This was a critical moment, as critical as those first few months in Canada. No matter the labour expended, no matter the energy given, it often was not enough to succeed. Whether because of poor or foolish financial decisions or simply the luck of the draw, the fact was that they had failed. A few chose to accept their fate, put the best face on it, and returned to the Netherlands with the hope that somehow they could reintegrate themselves. Yet many of those who went back home would return, feeling themselves, in the short period of absence, already isolated from the place of their birth.

Others turned in different directions. Temporarily hiring themselves out to other farmers, they began to look for opportunities outside the agricultural sector. The post-war baby boom and the growing industrialization and urbanization of the Canadian society pulled them, as it had other immigrants, to the growing cities. Unskilled workers of all kinds were needed to build the houses, pave the streets, and work in the factories. Although some had resisted the pull in the Netherlands, financial necessity now drove them into other occupations in Canada. Some farm immigrants, with skills in carpentry, masonry, and construction, began to use these skills in the new environment. Starting as labourers, many quickly worked themselves up to foremen and crew chiefs, eventually accumulating the experience and capital to begin tentatively on their own. Immigrants who had been permitted entry to fill specific demands for non-agricultural labour also prospered, some enjoying their work and reaping the financial benefits of their jobs with new cars and homes, and others seeing their employment as a way-station to better opportunities. They were joined by other immigrants who had merely regarded their one-year farm contracts as a temporary hindrance in their struggle to get on with their chosen occupations. Auto mechanics, bookkeepers, small businessmen, and tradesmen of all descriptions, who had found it necessary to rely on past agricultural experience in the Netherlands as an entry to Canada, now looked for an opportunity to return to familiar jobs.[13]

THE NEW BUSINESS

The physical and social isolation of the Dutch immigrants created new opportunities for those who had an entrepreneurial spirit and saw a chance to exercise it. One of the first to capitalize on the immigrants' lack of familiarity with, and sometimes dislike of, Canadian foodstuffs, household products, and other goods, and their lack of transportation was the travelling groceryman or peddler. Recognizing that the sale of imported or familiar goods to their fellow immigrants was a profitable venture, small businessmen established routes that would contact as many immigrants as possible. The travelling was often the result of necessity, as the basement store, warehouse, and office (all in one), no matter how well centred in concentrations of Dutch population, simply did not have sufficient customers to survive. Soon, jammed panel trucks rattled across every part of Canada.

The travelling grocer became a firmly established institution among the Dutch immigrants. Either importing the goods himself or purchasing from newly established importers in the larger cities, he provided a broad range of goods that made the adjustment to the new land that much easier. Dutch cigars, *hagelslag* (a sugar confection for bread), *appelstroop* (apple spread), cheese, *speculaas* (windmill cookies), textiles, and underwear (which wore longer and better than the Canadian variety, so it was claimed) made up only a small part of his stock.

Immigrants disappointed by Canadian bakery goods demanded imported honeycake, the familiar raisin bread, and assorted other confections. If the peddler could not supply the imported article he looked for someone in the Dutch community to provide it for him. Soon Dutch bakers, who had been forced by necessity either to work for others or to bake Canadian goods, turned to supplying a growing market among their compatriots.

While the groceryman generally did not have any kind of refrigeration, a demand existed for meat products. He turned to immigrant butchers to supply him with *rookwurst* (smoked sausage), *rookvlees* (smoked meat), and other prepared, non-perishable meat products. In areas of heavier Dutch concentration such as southern Ontario, where the business routes were shorter, the groceryman could carry Dutch cuts of meat cooled by a block of ice in a box. In such areas he often competed with other Dutch peddlers or with butchers who supplemented their incomes by the door-to-door sale of the cheap, and much desired, horsemeat. Besides horsemeat (smoked or fresh) these peddlers sold pork and the ever popular hamburger, which immigrant families could stretch to an unbelievable degree.

The visit of the groceryman was looked forward to with great expectation, particularly in rural areas. Besides his goods, he carried with him an enviable collection of news and gossip. He updated Canadian and Dutch events and reported on job opportunities and the condition of other immigrants. Dutch magazines such as *De Spiegel* (The Mirror) and *Panorama* appeared over the requisite cup of coffee or tea. While the ministers, priests, or fieldmen always had serious news, the peddler provided the spice of life along with a joke or two. In those areas where the routes were long and the groceryman was often on the road for days at a time, he was a welcome overnight visitor. No matter how crude the accommodation or severe the conditions the immigrants lived under, room could always be found and an extra potato provided. He always paid for his accommodation with goods from his truck. Eau de cologne for the lady of the house and *zoute drop* (salty licorice) or rolls of peppermints (without which, seemingly, no sermon could be endured) for the children were included without cost in the order. It was more than just shopping: it was a connection with the old country.

As more immigrants began to move into towns and urban centres and others acquired the wherewithal to purchase cars and trucks, the peddler saw his business begin to decline along his far-flung routes. The earlier isolation began to diminish but the need for his goods did not. The basement shop in his home, usually operated on a part-time basis by his wife or family in his absence, soon became too small to meet the growing demand. Not only were there more buyers, but as his clients struggled toward affluence, the list of goods demanded became greater. Peddling grew into a full-time established business, the "Dutch Store." As such businesses expanded they necessarily provided sales outlets for the Dutch bakers, butchers, and importers. What had begun as individual enterprise soon provided employment and opportunity for hundreds of others both in Canada and in the Netherlands.

The developing Dutch centres gave others opportunities to provide services to their fellow countrymen. Starting small, usually working out of the home or in the garage behind the house, small businessmen branched into every area of service. Bookkeepers, who by necessity had followed other professions on their arrival in Canada, soon began to work for other immigrants who had begun their own businesses. Mechanics began to supplement their incomes from their Canadian employers by repairing the cars and trucks of other immigrants. Booksellers imported reading material from the Netherlands and insurance salesmen used their contacts in the Dutch community to expand their businesses as the community became more affluent.

Every aspect of business came under the scrutiny of the immigrants and opportunities were exploited wherever possible, only limited by individual initiative and financial resources.[14]

NOTES

1. J. Vander Vliet to T. Cnossen, 29 December 1947, NESC, GAI.
2. Tuinman interview.
3. Nieboer interview.
4. *Ibid.*
5. Many immigrants have commented that while this settling-in period was the most difficult time of their lives, it was also the most exciting and of the deepest emotional intensity. The church and religion were seen as focal points for their emotional energies in both a religious and social sense.
6. Interview with Father Frank Ver Hagen, High River, Alberta, July, 1979.
7. J. Heersink, "The Canadian Work of the Reformed Church of America," 9 October 1952, John Heersink Papers.
8. A.S. Tuinman to N.E.F., 6 November 1947, NESC, GAI. The demand for workers in both the agricultural and industrial sectors brought about a scrambling for immigrants, which led to conflict between the Canadian departments of Labour and Mines and Resources since each wished to press its priority and control immigration.
9. A.S. Tuinman, "Report on 1948 Immigration," 22 February 1949, pp. 13-23, NESC, GAI.
10. For an excellent assessment of the role of Dutch agricultural immigrants in southwestern Ontario, see Anthony Sas, "Dutch Migration to and Settlement in Canada, 1945-1955," Ph.D. thesis, Clark University, 1957.
11. A.S. Tuinman to N.E.F., 14 December 1948, NESC, GAI; Ann van de Valk, "Dutch Immigration," brochure prepared by the Canadian Catholic Conference, 1947-48, NESC, GAI.
12. Stallinga interview.
13. Tuinman interview; Stallinga interview.
14. The material regarding the peddlers and other developing business enterprises is extracted from interviews and personal experience. The author accompanied his father on a horsemeat route and was personally acquainted with a number of grocery peddlers.

EIGHT

The Changing Fifties and Sixties

Changing conditions in the Netherlands and Canada greatly affected the character of the migration movement in the early 1950's. As Canada's economy began to diversify the government began to look with increasing favour on Dutch requests to expand the categories of admissible immigrants. Immigrants with skills in industry, construction, and services were needed to fill the growing demands of the non-agricultural sectors. Although the Netherlands was reluctant to see an exodus of highly skilled citizens, it did continue to urge the emigration of surplus factory workers, tradesmen, and small businessmen. In 1950 the new direction in immigration policy became apparent when only 34 per cent of the Dutch immigrants were classified as farm workers. From this time on, the new immigrants would take their place in all sectors of the Canadian economy.

In the Netherlands critical post-war problems were being taken in hand. Foreign aid, the rebuilding of industry, and the transformation and expansion of the economy were returning prosperity to the ravaged land. In 1953 the per capita income reached above the 1930 level for the first time and financial security and progress were on the horizon. The 1950's also saw the expansion of social welfare programs, labour and production reform, and the general bettering of social conditions. The expansion of available arable land due to a successful national program of reclamation provided more acreage for large farm families. The breakdown of social and provincial barriers and the rapid expansion of the Dutch economy made moving from the agricultural sector to urban occupations less difficult.

All these beneficial changes were not so apparent or obvious during the first four years of the fifties. These years saw the arrival in Canada of over 77,000 Dutch immigrants, more than twice as many as had arrived from 1945 to 1950. Increased Dutch subsidies to cover resettlement in Canada (from $2.5 million for 2,300 immigrants in 1950 to $27 million for 21,000 immigrants by 1953) and the devastating floods of 1953 continued to stimulate the movement. The old problems of lack of land, high population, unemployment, and shortage of housing persistently encouraged the idea of emigration. Both public and private emigration organizations, but particularly the private ones, were at their peak of efficiency and power and presented powerful reasons for overseas settlement. Without these organizations and their valuable connections in Canada the number emigrating would probably have been significantly smaller, especially in the latter half of the decade.

These emigrants were fortunate in having to face different circumstances from those of the immediate post-war years. Dutch monetary restrictions, which had prohibited the export of capital, were relaxed in 1954. With the introduction of passenger liners and direct air flights to Canada, the journey became less difficult. They also found that the Dutch-Canadian immigration societies were now functioning across the country and that placements were less haphazard and more successful. Dutch-Canadian communities were sprinkled across the land and often provided facilities and accommodation to welcome the new arrivals. The churches had been expanding in many new areas of the country, and as they grew the range of settlement possibilities increased. The base of the Dutch community developed by the pre-war immigrants and built upon by the post-war wave was now large enough to absorb readily the thousands of newcomers.

The arrival of the new immigrants also created a measure of division in the Dutch community. They seemed to be different from those who had preceded them in the late 1940's. Such a phenomenon was not new, as the early post-war immigrants were also different from those immigrants who had come before the Second World War. The "old-timers," as the pre-war immigrants were called, had found the new arrivals to be rather boisterous, uncontrolled, and not at all like themselves. The old-timers had been Canadianized in language and culture, particularly in such long-established settlements as Nobleford, Neerlandia, and Winnipeg. In some ways the early post-war immigrants were seen to act as foreigners, who had strange and often annoying peculiarities. They persisted, for example, in smoking in the church basement and meeting rooms; they seemed to have a rather liberal view toward the consumption of alcohol; and they gathered in noisy conclave before and after the services in the church. The old-timers forgot that times had changed in the Netherlands and, more importantly, that the church was also an important social institution, the one place where contact could be made. The immigrants did not have the wide social connections that were part of the old settlers' lives, and if they were boisterous and uncontrolled it was a result of their social isolation. In great measure grumbling was replaced with understanding or at least tolerance until new Canadian habits were inculcated and the rough edges were smoothed away.[1]

However, the new divisions in the 1950's were based on conflicts that were more than just cultural or social collisions between Dutch Canadians and Dutch immigrants. The new immigrants seemed to have more urban values and seemed less dedicated to the rural verities of large families, large farms, and economic self-sufficiency. Some even seemed to regard themselves as being innately better than the "farmers" who had arrived before them. The age-old suspicion of urban people by the rural populace was aggravated by the belated generosity of the Dutch government. The early post-war emigrants had virtually denuded themselves to find the cash to emigrate. The Dutch government, regarding farm workers as surplus, had been reluctant to grant financial subsidies, believing the movement would continue without aid. However, unemployment and lower-class standing in other sectors of the economy did not stimulate emigration to the extent that the agricultural crisis had. The government subsidies to these later emigrants naturally created jealousy in those who had come earlier.

These changing conditions, felt throughout the Dutch community, had some peculiar and noticeable effects on those Christian Reformed churches that served the old and the new immigrants, the rural and the urban. The church had had an important influence in settling and organizing the first wave of post-war immigration. In the Netherlands the state had provided money for separate schools, and as churches had been established for a significant number of years, finances were not a problem. Although a number of key churches were already established in Canada, they were insufficient for the membership and even they soon faced the financial burden of expansion. The struggle to maintain and develop the churches had been thrown on the immigrants. With sacrifice, the progression had been made from rented halls, to the purchase of land, to the building of temporary basement quarters, and finally, using communal labour, to the building of a church. While these sanctuaries were heavily mortgaged they stood as monuments to the dedication of the first post-war immigrants. The arrival of the new urban immigration presented issues that inevitably led to friction.

Some church members felt not only that the newcomers did not appreciate the difficulties that had been overcome but that they were too critical of the church leadership. During the first years the congregations, by necessity, had chosen deacons and elders from the available members. Class distinction and occupation, which had operated to some degree in the Netherlands in the choosing of church leaders, had been virtually wiped away under the pioneer conditions of early settlement. The predominance of American ministers and home missionaries had established, in some measure, a more democratic view, placing the emphasis on spirituality and experience. To some, the newcomers seemed to be trying to re-establish the dominance of the middle-class tradesmen and urbanites that had prevailed in the Netherlands. They resented this and conflict was the result. Such disputes exacerbated the discussion over other areas of church concern, such as physical expansion, the use of English in church services, the adoption of new hymns, and the establishment of Christian schools.

The earlier immigrants were by nature and training more conservative. They remembered the hardships and difficulties of providing money for ministers, missionaries, and new churches. Although the continual growth of the congregations seemed to indicate God's blessing on their past endeavours, they were reluctant to split the churches because of increasing membership. They were reluctant as well to build new churches, often deciding to make do with old facilities or simply to expand them. The newcomers, seeing the need, often pushed new development and expansion. Not until the ministers found the congregations too large to serve – physically and psychologically impossible to minister to – was there pressure from that area. Three or four services a day, limited parking space, and competition for meeting space often made the inconvenience factor so high that change became inevitable.

The use of English in church services was, as it had been in the pre-war churches, a contentious issue. The more conservative agricultural immigrant tended to see his language and religion as one package. However, the young people, quickly Canadianized in school and work and having no ongoing instruction in the Dutch language, soon pressed for the adoption of the English language in church services and related activities. They were supported in this effort by the ministers, often second- or third-generation Dutch Americans, and many of the newcomers. The newcomers often had some English-language training in schools, but more importantly they were more actively in contact with Canadians both at work and in their urban neighbourhoods. Unlike many Dutch-Canadian farmers, their social contacts included, by necessity as well as by chance or even choice, many English-speaking Canadians. Learning English and achieving proficiency in it were more important to them than to many rural immigrants. Less resistant to change and not sharing the conservative commitment to language and religion as one entity, they were prepared to make a rapid adaptation to the English language.

Since emigration and immigration organizations, and the Christian Reformed Church itself, stressed the necessity of learning the language and had expressed the belief that reformed Calvinism would only have an effect on Canadian society if it adopted the English language, the pressure from that direction was strong and consistent. Beginning with English catechism instruction and broadening into the young people's societies, the English language became accepted. Two-language sermons, with difficult English words being translated into Dutch, became the transitional method. After a few years even this became unnecessary as the language skills of the congregants increased. By the late 1950's and early 1960's most congregations limited themselves to one Dutch service a Sunday, and by the 1970's Dutch services were generally relegated to a few occasions, especially in the summer, when visitors from Holland might be attending.[2]

The issues surrounding a change of language also appeared in the Reformed Church of America and other reformed churches and can be seen largely as the result of a sometimes painful accommodation to the new culture. The first-generation agricultural immigrants were always most reluctant to give up the comfortable and known, but the growth of the churches made the change impossible to avoid. In the Reformed Church the passage was somewhat eased due to that church's contention that integration was not only welcome but necessary, and that its limited numbers demanded accommodation if the church was to survive in the larger Canadian society. Lack of members and churches seemed to necessitate the recruitment of Canadians to this church, unlike the numerically superior Christian Reformed Church.[3]

The Roman Catholic Church found itself spared this problem in that from the very beginning complete integration and assimilation were seen as the ultimate goal. Roman Catholic immigrants were to be incorporated into existing parishes. Church facilities and organizations already existed, thus sparing these immigrants organizational and financial problems. Furthermore, the Canadian bishops and the church hierarchy, often of Irish origin, wanted Dutch Canadians to settle in those rural parishes that had begun to shrink because of urbanization, and they rejected the concept of a "national" parish.[4]

By 1959 there were about eighty-five priests of Dutch origin, many belonging to missionary orders, working in Canada, but only six or seven were actively involved in the immigration movement and they served not only the Dutch but other immigrants as well. They encouraged English-language classes, involvement in church organizations, and the rapid acquisition of the English language. The Dutch-speaking priests wherever applicable gave the homily in the native language, made regular visits to their countrymen, did placements and helped with problems, and even on occasion held marathon Dutch-language confessionals. Due to their small numbers their tasks were immensely difficult and their labours were long and arduous. Their concern and encouragement were deeply appreciated by their parishioners as they made the difficult but necessary change to English.

The conservatism and sectarian separation of the Christian Reformed from the larger Dutch community created a number of other problems unique to that group. With the adoption of the English language in the church services, the issue of hymns made its appearance. When many of the early post-war immigrants left the Netherlands, their church hymnal consisted of the 150 Psalms set to music and twenty-nine other hymns based on biblical themes. The adoption of English meant the acceptance of the Christian Reformed Church of America Hymnal, which contained, among others, English and non-Dutch hymns of praise. Some ultra-conservative immigrants considered such hymns, if not unbiblical, at least the product of the seemingly unreformed society in which they found themselves. Stern opposition continued for a number of years against the incorporation of such songs in the church service and was expressed in refusal to stand and sing and in occasional walkouts and boycotts of church services. Such expressions of opposition had also been seen in the struggle against church expansion and the use of the English language and would be used to object to the push for Christian schools. It took all the diplomatic skills of the ministers and the consistories and sometimes even the discipline of the church to effect a change of attitude among the objectors, but eventually the new hymns were accepted as part of the religious services.

The struggle over the Christian school issue was often as contentious and disruptive as the other issues had been. While there was a consensus that the public schools in Canada were not neutral but taught values in opposition to Christian Reformed principles, many disagreed as to how their children should be taught. Generally, the members of the Christian Reformed Church opposed such worldly amusements as movie attendance, card-playing, and dancing, entertainments the public schools either ignored, promoted, or made no moral judgement on. The question of public school education went deeper, however. These schools, while teaching nominal religious sentiments, gave no moral instruction and failed to recognize the supremacy of God in all life. The most blatant example of this omission was the teaching of evolution. As a result, some believed that an attempt should be made to change the existing public schools into more reformed institutions. Given the constraints of language and numbers, however, this seemed to be an impractical position. Others objected to the separatism implied by a parallel school system. A significant number of others believed that whatever the shortcomings of the Canadian public school system, deficiencies could be remedied by home instruction and the guidance and help of the church.

The real issue, however, was the question of money. Congregations already burdened by the high costs of building and expansion were sometimes reluctant, and often unable, to find the funds for school buildings, teachers, and transportation. Although school societies run by parents were by constitution and practice independent of the Christian Reformed Church, in actual fact the membership of the two organizations was often the same, and the same pockets had to be emptied for both. The necessity was there, but the financial burden to provide an alternative "Christian" education seemed insurmountable.

The financially conservative element in the church adopted a go-slow attitude while some 30 per cent of the congregation pushed for the establishment of their own schools. In some cases this fractured the church communities, with ministers occasionally falling between the contending parties. The fact that in the Netherlands the state supported the Christian schools encouraged some lobbying for provincial support, while others regarded the privately supported system of Christian Reformed schools in the United States as the model for Canadian development. Some school societies began building in prayer and hope while others waited until adequate financing was available. The continued growth of the Christian Reformed communities and the commitment to a God-centred, quality education for the whole Canadian community, based on reformed traditions, eventually led to a nationwide system of Christian elementary and high schools in all the provinces except Newfoundland, where there had been little Christian Reformed settlement.[5]

While the Christian Reformed Church, as the largest Dutch-Canadian church, perhaps most obviously exemplifies some of the conflicts that erupted in the religious life of the Dutch-Canadian community, it was not unique in its experience. Religion and its practice were central to a great number of immigrants, and the church was bound to become the conduit for the streams of change that affected the immigrant community. It was on the front line of cultural adaptation and as such mirrored the desires, fears, and problems of the immigrants.

THE FRACTURED COMMUNITY

The differing views held by new immigrants about the problems they faced mirrored the divisions that had separated them at home. Now these divisions reappeared in their new homeland. Such divisions were not so much a matter of conscious choice as they were dictated by long-standing habits and views. With the church as one of the primary instruments of community formation, the immigrants were naturally divided along religious lines. Older Protestant or Catholic immigrants of the pre-war settlement would not employ fellow countrymen of contrary religious affiliation. The deep suspicion of Romanism among the Protestant groups merely exacerbated the provincial or regional differences that had also always existed among the Dutch. Social contact was limited to chance meetings and no real measure of understanding was achieved, or even desired, between the two groups. The fact that all were Dutch immigrants in a strange land did nothing to encourage any group homogeneity.[6]

As the Roman Catholics began to integrate into Canadian society, contacts with other immigrants tended to diminish even further. Since intermarriage between Dutch Catholics and Dutch Protestants was undesirable, kinship contacts were not established between the two alienated groups. Roman Catholic views, more liberal toward movies, drinking, card-playing, and other secular pleasures, alienated them further from the more orthodox Reformed community. In line with the *zuilen* principle as established in the Netherlands, the Roman Catholics regarded themselves as distinctly different from other Dutch immigrants. This difference was clearly seen in the establishment of the Catholic religious journal *Onder Ons* (Among Us), which later became known as *Compass*. It was a publication dedicated to the integration and easing of Dutch Roman Catholics into Canadian society.[7] Clearly, Canada was not a place where the rifts of religious diversity were to be healed.

As with the relations between Catholics and Protestants, the Reformed and Christian Reformed communities found themselves separated by social and religious distance. Although contacts seemed to be somewhat easier, due to some intermarriage and an almost imperceptible trickle of more liberal and less dogmatic people from the Christian Reformed Church to the Reformed, the groups existed side by side in relative isolation from each other. The smallness of the Reformed Church community tended to make it more susceptible to the adoption of Canadian lifestyles and attitudes, and this further weakened the bond of Dutchness that might have held the groups together in a kind of tolerant relationship. As it was, this distance encouraged each group to establish parallel churches in the Dutch community with competing young peoples', women's, and men's societies and church magazines.[8]

The Reformed Church in America established the *Pioneer* as its Canadian complement to its American church magazine, the *Church Herald*. The Christian Reformed Church created a church newspaper, the *Calvinist Contact*. It also encouraged an established American-Dutch church newsletter,

De Wachter, to include Canada in its coverage. Besides the *Calvinist Contact* and *De Wachter*, the Christian Reformed Church also published the English-language *Banner*, which was primarily aimed at the American congregations. The *Pioneer* and the *Calvinist Contact* were bilingual and carried church news, discussion of conditions in Holland and in Canada, advice for immigrants, ongoing series, advertisements from Dutch-Canadian businessmen, community and church announcements, poems, and religious articles and messages.

The separation between the two religious groups, as in the Netherlands, extended to every aspect of life. In the late 1950's and early 1960's some tolerance did develop. This was largely due to the second-generation immigrants' failure to understand or accept the religious arguments that separated the churches. This more easy relationship did not, however, extend to church union, although it did lead to co-operation in the support of Christian mental hospitals, rehabilitation centres, and other worthwhile causes. This would lead to the exchange of pulpits on Sundays by visiting ministers or pulpit supply when a church had a ministerial vacancy. Easier contact between the young was also initiated on the organizational level, particularly in those areas where marriage partners were less readily available for the Reformed Church members.[9]

The Christian Reformed Church, although the largest Dutch church in Canada with 192 congregations and affiliated Christian elementary and high schools, should itself not be regarded as free from religious division. The reforming impulse inherent in Calvinism has made itself clearly felt in that church. Following the development and expression of Calvinist thought in the Netherlands, as an example, a minority of Christian Reformed people (perhaps 20 per cent) have sought to impress reformed principles on Canadian society. Taking as their credo that human life in its entirety is religion, they have attempted to make their Calvinism relevant to the society around them. This group was involved in the founding of the Association for Reformed Scientific Studies in 1956 and began an earnest drive to establish a Reformed university on the North American continent, specifically in Canada. Out of this organization has developed the Association for the Advancement of Christian Scholarship, which operates the Institute for Christian Studies in Toronto. This institute offers graduate university programs that "aim to help people develop a Christian understanding of their studies and life-work."[10]

The belief that all activity must "heed the normative direction of God's word, acknowledge His law to which creation in all its spheres is subject and will bow before Christ's kingship" had led proponents of this idea into new directions in Canadian society. They have established the Christian Labour Association of Canada, an alternative to secular unionism, the Christian Farmer's Association, and the Citizens for Public Justice. While the impact of these organizations has been strong on the Christian Reformed community, although not without dissension and conflict, it has not been great on the larger Canadian community. These organizations have, however, made Canadians somewhat more aware of the Christian Reformed Church as an organization that seems to hold ideas in opposition to prevailing liberal and secular thinking.

The reforming impulse was, however, not always contained within the Christian Reformed Church. Conflicts over the matters of common grace, the Church Order, and other doctrinal matters, which had been so much a part of the Dutch experience, spilled over into Canada. While a sense of unity in the face of adversity restrained argument in the first few years of settlement, by the beginning of the 1950's old differences once again rose to the surface. Some orthodox Calvinists who had temporarily aligned them-selves with the Christian Reformed Church as a matter of religious conve-nience began to give expression to the doctrinal differences that had sepa-rated them into competing churches in the Netherlands. Oftentimes this led to open conflict resulting in the withdrawal of the dissenting minority from the established churches.

Such disagreements led to the founding of the Canadian Reformed Church in 1950. This church, taking its theological direction from a reformist move-ment that had developed in the Netherlands during the Second World War, based its position on a more literal belief in the Bible and saw itself as more diligently reformed in nature. Generally referred to as "Article 31" (relating to the Church Order), it is regarded as more conservative than the Christian Reformed Church. After thirty years of existence this church is composed of twenty-nine congregations, predominantly in British Columbia and the West, and has a separate Christian school system and a seminary in Hamilton, Ontario.[11]

Another conservative outgrowth of the Christian Reformed Church has been the Free Christian Reformed Church. Founded in 1955, this church is composed of twelve congregations. As it has no seminary, it trains its minis-ters at the Christian Reformed seminary in Grand Rapids, Michigan.

The Netherlands Reformed Congregation, today composed of twelve churches, is the most conservative of all the Reformed churches. Called the "black-stockings" because of their predilection for plain dress, they avoid most secular pleasures. The doctrines of the church heavily emphasize the existence of an omniscient and omnipotent God and the sinful and depraved nature of man. Their theology has been called the "dour theology," as it emphasizes the restricted nature of salvation. This church found itself in the public eye during the late 1970's as a result of its opposition to immunization against polio because its followers regard such an action as thwarting the will of an all-powerful God. Limited in numbers, this church recruits its ministers from the Netherlands.[12]

Although all the Reformed churches have a common origin in the Nether-lands, contact between the groups is generally limited. Some attempts have been made to discuss church union between the Reformed Church and the Christian Reformed Church, but these efforts have had little success in spite of the churches' co-operation in other areas. Discussions between the Chris-tian Reformed Church and the Canadian Reformed Church have also failed to reach any substantive agreement in spite of the fact that some Canadian Reformed send their children to the Christian Reformed schools. The ideological segregation that has bound the groups in place in the Netherlands clearly has been re-established in Canada, and there is little hope that such division can be ended in the near future.

THE URBAN ADJUSTMENT

Although the integration of the non-agricultural Dutch immigrant into the Canadian society was eased by the existing organizations and institutions established by the previous immigrants, it was, nevertheless, difficult.[13] While this had been expected by both the Canadian and Dutch officials and even the immigrants themselves, no amount of preparation and warning could isolate these immigrants from the personal crises that resulted from the cultural and social disruption of the move. Getting used to Canadian work methods in the factory or office was as difficult as it had been on the farm. For the first year everything was truly strange and often threatening, and some, because of easier economic and transportation circumstances, returned to the Netherlands. The overwhelming majority, however, chose to stick it out.

The newly arrived immigrants' entry into the urban work force meant a broader contact with English Canadians than had been possible for the agricultural immigrants. Readier access to night school and a greater necessity to use English encouraged faithful attendance at English-language classes for both men and women. The physical isolation that agriculturalists had experienced was broken down for the urban immigrants by their residency in city neighbourhoods.

While the new immigrants did not consciously congregate in specific urban areas, financial necessity often forced them to live in low-cost areas. Accumulating the capital to achieve financial security necessitated prudent decisions. It was generally agreed that it was better to live cheaply for a while and save money than to make a precipitous plunge into something that was financially unwise. The result of such a decision was an immediate sprucing up, painting, and repairing of the available facilities. Paint, scrub brush, and rake accomplished a lot, even in rented quarters. Canadian landlords came to regard the Dutch immigrants as good tenants and the Canadian neighbours were reassured that the stereotypical "clean" Dutchman really did exist.

The struggle for financial security touched the urban immigrants as deeply as it had the rural ones. With the ready availability of bus or other transportation, women quickly capitalized on the crying need for domestic help. The Dutch cleaning lady became much sought after among well-to-do Canadians. For a dollar an hour for an eight-hour day, lunch, and transportation, the Dutch penchant for cleanliness was brought into Canadian homes. Immigrant women did not consider such labour demeaning since they were contributing to the financial health of the family. House-cleaning was often difficult because of the lack of available transportation or the exacting demands of the employer. The call for cleaning ladies was, however, so great that troublesome clients could be dropped and more accommodating ones accepted.

Such work brought not only money but other benefits as well. Women had an opportunity to leave the neighbourhood and lessen their loneliness by coming in contact with people outside their own small circle. The English language was more easily acquired and they were introduced to Canadian cooking and family life. New recipes for such dishes as squash, corn, and macaroni casseroles were brought home to try on the family, not always with a favourable reception. Perhaps most importantly, a new awareness grew of the social and material benefits the new society offered.

The cleaning lady could not help but notice the material comfort of her clients nor fail to comment on the wasteful disposal of leftover food or repairable items. Subtle hints about the financial difficulties of immigrant life and the generosity of the employer often resulted in the gift of used items and discarded clothing. Dresses, suits, and particularly children's clothes were eagerly accepted since they helped to defray the costs in the immigrant home. Employers were also often generous with advice, recommendations for jobs for some member of the family, financial aid in times of trouble, and loans for the purchase of a car, home, or the starting of a business. Bonds of friendship, concern, and a deeper understanding between immigrants and Canadians sometimes resulted from this, initially at least, purely financial arrangement.

In spite of the benefits of such employment, it brought with it a heavy burden for the women. Canada presented problems that every immigrant housewife had to contend with. The problems of transportation and a new language made shopping difficult. Rather than shopping every day in neighbourhood markets as in the Netherlands, the housewife made a weekly trip to the supermarket where she was faced with a confusing display of goods. The language on the packages was unfamiliar and choice was often made on the basis of the picture, with sometimes unwelcome results. The cuts of meat were different than at home and prepared meats, a staple of the Dutch breakfasts and lunches, neither looked nor tasted like the ones she was familiar with, particularly if they contained garlic. Canadian cheese, primarily cheddar, bore no resemblance to Edam, Gouda, or Leyden cheese in texture, flavour, or colour. Fresh vegetables and fruit, so common in the Netherlands due to greenhouse cultivation, seemed in Canada to be largely seasonal and presented only a few choices. Bakery products, like vegetables, were limited in selection and consisted mostly of bread and pies and some sweet rolls. All in all, it appeared difficult unless one went to the Dutch store (another trip) to approximate the Dutch cuisine. But at least food was relatively cheap, compared to that in the Netherlands, and the supply of staples was more than abundant. A certain amount of accommodation was required and made.

Household tasks also necessitated some adjustments. Learning to cook on electric stoves in some areas, rather than on gas, and finding that some Canadian homes had no built-in wash tubs for the laundry presented some difficulties. On the other hand, washing machines, vacuum cleaners, and other household appliances, usually purchased second-hand, greatly lightened the workload. Employment as a cleaning lady in a Canadian household quickly convinced many women of the necessity of such "luxuries" and gave them an easy familiarity with them. The adjustment for women was probably more comprehensive than for their husbands and families, but given a little help from friends and employers it could be achieved.

As the mother was usually home by the time the children got back from school there was seldom a serious disruption of family life. Such employment for two or three days a week no doubt encouraged the children, when they came of age, to look for ways they could supplement the family income. Newspaper routes were avidly sought after, as were sidewalk shovelling, lawn-mowing, cleaning up, and numerous other jobs. Part-time jobs in service stations and businesses of all kinds, and helping Father on Saturdays or evenings with a small business or job he had on the side, provided pocket money and an introduction to possible future employment. Girls sometimes joined their mothers in housekeeping work, when they were not at school. Their willingness to work often contrasted sharply with that of their Canadian peers, and employers were impressed by the perseverance and energy of the immigrant children.

Such orientation to work sometimes meant neglect of educational opportunities since many children, like their parents, regarded economic security as a primary goal. Many left school, often by their own choice, to pursue more immediate economic rewards. Most made a success of their endeavours through hard work and ingenuity. For many it meant a succession of jobs and learning skills until finally they found permanent positions. Their desire for achievement was generally rewarded by their employers, and a Dutchman was considered a "hard worker" who merited a little extra chance or money. The relative financial success of these first-generation children attests to their willingness to get the job done. Unfortunately, it has also led to some personal dissatisfaction in later life with the apparent emptiness of material success.

The strong family orientation among both the rural and urban immigrants meant that women regarded employment outside the home as temporary or only part-time. Young women usually did not envision a career outside of the family. Jobs were taken either to supplement family income or to purchase the necessary equipment for the home. Marriage, raising children, and caring for the husband were seen as the proper goals for a woman, by both women and men. In difficult times a woman might have to work in the labour force, but it was generally assumed that being a housewife was a full-time occupation. Higher education, with the possible exception of teacher training, was often seen as unnecessary and perhaps dangerous as it could lead to serious conflicts in the family.

The growing contacts of family members in the larger Canadian community sometimes provided new opportunities in business development. Casting about for ways to earn extra income, immigrants noticed the need for gardeners to cut lawns, look after flower beds, and do yardwork. Since the Dutch had the reputation for having "green thumbs" and the initial investment was quite low (a lawn mower, rake, shovel and spade, and a pair of clippers), a new enterprise was founded. Such businesses, begun part-time after factory or construction work was finished, sometimes blossomed into full-time occupations. First customers were often the owners of the homes that were cleaned by the mother of the family or a friend.

Contacts of this nature sometimes permitted an urban family either to return to or to begin a limited farming enterprise. Some immigrants felt cooped up in the city or in factory jobs and simply wanted to get out on their own. With careful saving they were able to acquire a small acreage where they could grow vegetables and keep a few chickens. Keeping their city jobs, they sold eggs and vegetables to Canadians and fellow countrymen on a regular route basis. The Dutch eggman is still a common sight in some urban areas and his part-time job has become a full-time occupation.

Finances presented a severe problem to the immigrants in those years. It was not simply a matter of having enough but also of how the money was used and invested. Starting in the 1890's in the Netherlands, co-operative savings and lending institutions had been developed, often along religious lines. The small saver and borrower, farmer or urbanite, had sought an alternative to the large banking institutions, which had virtually ignored him. On arriving in Canada the immigrants once again found themselves the victims of a disinterested banking system.

Organizing on religious lines, Protestant and Catholic, and even on non-denominational lines such as DUCA Community Credit Union of Toronto (founded 1954), Dutch immigrants developed credit unions to meet their needs. Beginning as savings institutions, often in someone's basement, these credit unions expanded, as capital and banking laws allowed, to full-service financial institutions. Their basis was co-operative, the language used was Dutch, the profit was shared, and, more importantly, the loans were provided on the basis of reputation and ability. St. Willibrod Credit Union of London, the second largest credit union in Ontario today, was started by Dutch and Flemish Roman Catholics in 1951. Other Dutch credit unions had their beginnings among members of the Reformed community. Whatever their origin, all now serve the larger Canadian community and are monuments to the success of the co-operative movement.

It is noteworthy as well that some Dutch-Canadian businessmen, although getting their start in the Dutch community and depending on their fellow countrymen for their initial business, have not remained isolated from the larger Canadian society. The reputation for ambitious and honest hard work, which they shared with the other Dutch immigrants, led them into the broader Canadian business world.

The Dutch immigrant of the 1950's, like so many other immigrants to Canada, turned his hand to whatever occupation offered him a chance to succeed. No job was too menial or too hard if it was potentially profitable. Factory or farm, service or construction, each had its own unique opportunities and, sometimes, difficulties. One such difficulty, particularly for orthodox

Calvinists, lay with the Canadian unions. While the Dutch were not opposed to unions *per se*, they were opposed to "secular unions" that believed in class struggle and confrontation between employers and employees. Christian labour unions or associations had been founded in the Netherlands at the turn of the century. They stressed co-operation and discussion based on Christian principles and brotherly love, not confrontation. Canadian unions were, however, confrontation-oriented and had little use, seemingly, for the principles of Dutch Calvinists. Whether or not to belong to a secular union became a serious question for these immigrants in the 1950's.

Many Reformed churches pointed out the inconsistency between union membership and the Calvinist life. While some regarded the shunning of secular unions as a sign of faith, others left it to individual conscience. This conscience became most apparent in places of employment where unionization was undertaken after employment had already begun. Some refused to join the union and lost their jobs; others refused to pay union dues and instead donated the money to charity, leading to their eventual firing. Still others helped organize the Christian Labour Association of Canada, which lobbies for the open-shop union concept where union membership is a matter of personal choice. The Christian Labour Association also functions as a labour union, usually for Dutch-Canadian employers.

The opposition to secular unions has led to charges of naiveté, stupidity, and union- and strike-breaking by Canadian unionists when Dutch-Canadian Calvinists have refused to support what they regard as immoral strikes. In the main, the issue of union membership has been determined by financial necessity and the majority of Dutch-Canadian Calvinists have bowed to the Canadian reality. There have been some, however, who could not in good conscience support the unions and as a result have suffered economically for their beliefs. Others have benefited in that employers who have wanted to avoid union disruption have sought them out.

Sunday labour presented another difficulty for many immigrants. On the farm, arrangements could often be made with the employer. General farm work was not done, although animals were fed and cows were milked. If Sunday labour was necessary to get in the crop, it was generally not done by Calvinist employees but by the Canadian farmer himself. In the city, however, and particularly in the factory, such arrangements were not easy to make. Shift work often entailed Sunday labour as the machines could not be permitted to stand idle. Trading work days with fellow employees was one way to handle the problem, but this was not always possible. Refusing to work on Sunday generally led to being fired, and since many orthodox Calvinists regarded such labour as prohibited by the Ten Commandments, they accepted their fate. As with union membership, the decision was a difficult one, balanced as it was between personal conscience and economic need.

Opposition to Sunday labour also meant the avoidance of doing any business on Sunday. No gasoline, food, household necessities, or other purchases were made if they could possibly be avoided. Only a dire necessity or emergency would force a Dutch Calvinist to ask someone else to work on Sunday for him. Even the discussion of business matters that would entail the future transfer of money was frowned upon. The Sabbath was regarded by many as a holy day. While union membership and Sunday observance were often critical problems for the orthodox Calvinists, they presented less difficulty to other immigrants who had a more pragmatic view of financial necessity or a less legalistic religious view.

INTERMARRIAGE

Soon after their arrival, Dutch immigrants were faced with an unforeseen result of their immigration to Canada, which was to create great consternation and conflict. This was the matter of intermarriage with Canadians. The Roman Catholics were probably the first group to have to face this problem to any great extent, for they were the most integrated of the Dutch immigrants. Their involvement and inclusion in the Canadian church and its organizations had rapidly brought them into proximity with the new society. Although they tended to retain close contact with other Dutch Roman Catholics, their social group extended to include the non-Dutch. Their children had been absorbed into Catholic schools and youth organizations and most of their social contacts were Canadian. The result of this mixing at first was friendships and then love interest, which the Dutch parents sometimes found hard to accept.

This lack of acceptance usually did not lie with the religious issue but was rather a matter of family needs and preferences and occasionally national or racial prejudices. For, despite their apparent integration in the larger Catholic community, Dutch Catholics like other Dutch Canadians remained very Dutch. The language, customs, and attitudes in the home were Dutch, and the appearance of an English Canadian in the family would mean someone completely unfamiliar with their style of life. Communication would be difficult, foods different, and, most importantly, the nature of family relations would be changed. Canadian families were perceived as being less patriarchal and authoritarian than the Dutch, and as a result the strong influence the father or the parents had exerted over the family would be diminished. In reality, opposition to marriage outside the group was based on the fear of the unknown, and parents preferred their children to marry other Catholic Dutch Canadians.

Dutch-Canadian parents, regardless of religious conviction, also sometimes based their objections on national differences that were simply prejudicial in nature. Dutch Canadians often regarded other Canadians of eastern and southern European extraction as inferior to themselves. The substantial hatred of Germans, which had grown out of the last war, made alliances with this group particularly objectionable. Blacks, Indians, and Asians were simply unacceptable. The most acceptable of the non-Dutch were Canadians of western European origin, particularly from the British Isles. While objections died slowly, parents were faced with the inevitable fact that, in Canada, children were less prone to obey their parents in such matters and that marriages took place with or without their agreement. Cultural differences did place roadblocks in the way of achieving stable marriages, but failure was not inevitable, and grandchildren soon took the sting out of what had seemed to be an unhappy choice. Accommodations could be made, if necessary, from both sides.

Other Dutch immigrants voiced many of the same objections to intermarriage that had been put forward by the Roman Catholics, but as long as the issue of religion did not raise its head there was no concerted effort to oppose it. However, among the Christian Reformed and more orthodox Calvinists it was seen as a genuine danger to the faith and strongly opposed on that basis. Marriage outside the group was undesirable as it was felt that the non-Reformed partner would lead the other person out of the faith. If the Canadian was brought into the church prior to the marriage it was more acceptable, but still dangerous. Organizations such as young people's groups and clubs, as well as the Christian school and such institutions of higher learning as the Christian Reformed Calvin College in Grand Rapids, Michigan, were seen as means of broadening the social circle and encouraging marriage within the group. Church refusal to marry people who were not of the same faith and family pressure helped to curb the intermarriage rate. Although there was little intermarriage among the Reformed in the 1950's, it would increase as the children of immigrants became more and more Canadianized.

THE COST

Dutch immigrants, whatever their social or religious origin, shared a belief in the work ethic, which taught not only the virtue of labour but also the necessity of overcoming the difficulties standing in the way of economic independence. Success was measured by material achievement: a farm, a home, a car, or even perhaps a business of one's own. By the late fifties, such measurements indicated that the Dutch had been successful in their immigration to Canada, but they failed to show the human and personal costs exacted for such welfare.

Clergymen who worked among the immigrants quickly became aware of the prominence money and material things began to assume. It was not merely that church donations often seemed to fall below realistic levels or that Christian schools were sometimes regarded as expensive fripperies, but *geld-zucht* (money lust) seemed to be a growing peril. Community involvement, personal development and growth, even family needs were often subservient to the desire to get ahead. Such single-mindedness left many victims in its wake.

Financial necessity often created situations that were to plague human relations for years to come. Underbidding for work against other immigrants was regarded by some as an underhanded gesture that stole the bread from another's mouth. Solidarity against employers who wanted the lowest possible wage was forgotten in the desire to get ahead and many justified their action simply as good business sense. Such activity crossed religious and ethnic lines, creating mistrust and anger not only in the Dutch community but also against it by other ethnic groups. It is not difficult to understand that some Dutch immigrants came to acquire the reputation of slick operators who were so dedicated to money-grubbing that even friendship could be cast away.

While clergymen railed against the dedication to Mammon that short-changed the social aspects of life, they were more concerned about the personal, spiritual, and familial effects. Long hours of work, while often necessary in the first years of settlement, became habitual even when economic security was achieved. Such work precluded service in church offices, involvement in church organizations, and even Sunday attendance. English-language instruction was often ignored, not because it was unnecessary but in the belief that acquiring money was more important than learning the language of the new country. Increasingly, many of the first-generation immigrants became loners, sometimes separated even from their own families by the demands of their personal struggle.

Such isolation led to problems that at times threatened the strongly family-centred Dutch-Canadian society. Authoritarian in nature and patriarchal in design, the families took their direction from the father's wishes. This power, supported at least in the Calvinist community by the ethic of the sovereign God-Father and the commandment to honour one's father and mother, was often wielded with devastating effect. Wives were expected to be submissive and bow to the will of their husbands. Such obedience often meant giving up social contacts because of work or moving to new areas that promised greater financial rewards. Such changes of residence, whether to new farms or into the city, often shattered newly established friendships and social circles. This uprooting was particularly difficult for those women who had limited social interaction outside their families and who feared having to establish new friendships in a new environment.

The demands of success sometimes saw the mother aligned with the father against children who questioned the cost of the immigrant venture. Forced to leave school at the age of fourteen, they were directed into practical work that would make them self-sufficient and the family a viable economic unit. Although such pressure was most often seen among farmers, it was also evident among urban immigrants. As the society surrounding them became more technical and diversified, the necessity of higher education forced a reassessment of the practice of early school leaving. The seemingly limitless opportunities available to the less well-educated were disappearing in the late fifties and high school and university were seen as possibilities, even necessities. As their eyes remained on the opportunity to get ahead, more consideration was given to further education in both rural and urban areas. Technical training in agriculture and trades was taken up, as were apprenticeship programs. Vocational education in high schools was stressed for both boys and girls in preparing them for the work world. This practical view of education extended to the university level, where immigrant children moved into such job-oriented programs as education, commerce, engineering, and social work. The sheer pleasure of learning took second place to pragmatic financial considerations.

Those who were able to attend university were the lucky ones, for some, despite their desire, had to submit to wishes of parents who felt that education had a limited usefulness. The family unit was stressed as the source and goal of loyalty and support. Children were sometimes directed into the most lucrative positions despite their own desires. Many laboured for years, putting off marriage, families, education, or personal predilections in order to establish the family farm or business. Inevitably, this kind of submission led to feelings of personal worthlessness, anger at parents, and distrust of others, whom they perceived as being motivated solely by self-interest. Families broke up as members sought to go their own way, often without the blessing or financial support of the unit they had struggled to establish. Disobedience to parents led to bitterness from both sides, hostility among siblings, and the guilt of failure.

Such feelings of failure and inferiority were also evident among some immigrant children as they sought to make the adjustment to the Canadian society. The school and the neighbourhood were sometimes perceived as being alien and they felt themselves to be unhappily peculiar. Different styles of dress (knickers and woollen undershirts) were immediately noticeable. Having been placed back in grades and having difficulty with the language made it hard for them to become part of the group. The obvious financial disparity precluded sharing many of the things Canadian children took for granted. Parent-teacher meetings became occasions for embarrassment as the language gap was emphasized. Caught between two worlds, obedient to parents and teachers, some children found themselves barely coping with the demands placed on them. Added to this was their parents' often barely concealed distrust of foreigners (Canadians), which the children recognized but were unable to deal with.

Frustration could also often lead to the same excessive zeal to achieve that motivated their parents, but it, too, had its drawbacks. Success at school pleased parents and teachers alike, but it could alienate the peer group to which they so badly wished to belong. The prohibition on going to movies, dancing, and card-playing or the use of cosmetics further separated many Calvinist children from their schoolmates. Traditional disapproval of sports as a waste of useful energy and time only furthered the distance.

Many children came to resent and hate the "Dutchness" of their parents, their lack of skill with the English language, their alien customs and religion. These were seen as things to be disposed of in the struggle to become more Canadian. The conflict raged in every area, from dress to food, to attitudes about dating and even names. To some, everything about their parents was old-fashioned, objectionable, and Dutch. Why were their parents unable or unwilling to accommodate themselves? What was wrong with corn, squash, and apple pie or a Canadian Christmas? Who needed to go to church twice on Sunday or catechism or all those youth organizations? Canadians were more enlightened, more advanced, and to be Canadian was better than to be a "stupid immigrant."

Parents faced with this kind of conflict increasingly held on to what was familiar and understood. Life in the homeland took on a rosier hue. Yet, by the act of immigration they had separated themselves from the changes that were continuing in Dutch society, and return became more difficult even if it was financially possible. Many Calvinists rejected what they regarded as dangerous liberal tendencies in Canadian society. Although Catholics were to have fewer difficulties, certainly on the religious level, even their ideas of social relations and family solidarity were threatened upon occasion. But their rapid involvement in the Canadian church and society made the transition from one culture to another much easier for their children and even for themselves. The Canadian Catholic Church provided the warmth, lessened the loneliness, and made the acceptance of new traditions and ideas much easier for them than for the Calvinists, who had already been separated from the mainstream of society in the Netherlands. No matter the religious or social origin, the children of immigrants often found an accommodation difficult, however much desired.

Although most children accepted the wishes of their parents and maintained the solidarity of the family and their community above their own needs, some openly rebelled, breaking the rules and earning the anger and confusion of their parents. Leaving home as early as possible, they struck out on their own and attempted to Canadianize themselves as much as possible. Sometimes changing their names to make them less foreign sounding, they refused to speak Dutch or have anything to do with the community from which they had come.

Most, however, made their accommodation, neither rebelling nor completely acquiescing. They made friends in both communities and became as Canadian as possible while still recognizing their origins. Dancing, drinking, card-playing, or movie-going was done on the sly. Marriage might occasionally be outside the group for Calvinists and more often for Roman Catholics, but they tended to stick with the familiar. They were confident that when they were on their own they could accommodate themselves to the extent that was comfortable and acceptable to themselves. In this process they made the kinds of changes many other immigrant groups had undertaken to become part of the Canadian society.

Most children found that change was unavoidable, even for their parents, as they slowly became more and more Canadian – trying new foods, becoming less restrictive in their social relations, changing dress and customs to keep up with the altered conditions of their family and children. Even the most reluctant were forced to change, if only to the point of admitting that not all of Canadian society, customs, manners, or habits were objectionable. Many came to believe that:

> . . . the immigrant must go beyond negative criticism. He must have a basic interest in the true welfare of his new country and of his fellow

countrymen. He must seek to approach them with a friendliness that is not camouflaged self-interest, but a genuine concern for them as individuals with whom he would share a heritage. He must ever prove the sincerity of his approach with a friendliness that is eager to give what he has. Let him pave the road of integration with solid service. The way seems arduous and long, but as he works he finds that he feels less and less like a "stranger in a strange land." His new countrymen watch him work, and they judge the same.[14]

The improving conditions in the Netherlands in the late 1950's and the growing complexity of the Canadian economy increasingly discouraged the migration of the relatively unskilled and untrained. In 1955 Dutch immigration dropped from a previous high of 16,300 in 1954 to 7,000. Although there was a resurgence in 1957 to over 12,000 people, caused by a recession and the fear of Communist aggression growing out of the Hungarian revolution of 1956, Dutch immigration to Canada was never again to reach the proportions it had in the decade following the end of the Second World War.[15] By 1960 the number had dropped to 6,600 people.

The expansion of available arable land due to a successful national program of reclamation in the Netherlands provided more acreage for the large farm families that had previously been inclined to emigrate. The breakdown of social and provincial barriers due to modern communications media and the rapid expansion of the Dutch economy's industrial sector made moving from rural to urban occupations less difficult. The size of families declined even in the rural areas, as birth control became more acceptable with the increasing liberalization of the Dutch churches. In fact, by 1959 the Dutch government came under some pressure to curtail emigration activities because a labour shortage was developing. By 1960 there seemed to be less and less reason for the Dutch to leave their newly prosperous little homeland.

The declining immigration had both positive and negative effects on the Dutch-Canadian community. The immigration societies that had been so busy in the past now found their responsibilities steadily declining. As a result, the job of fieldman became largely redundant and voluntary assistance replaced that remunerated position. Local immigration organizations simply disappeared and those owning immigrant homes sold them and dispersed the funds. The decline in numbers aided the Anglicization of the community, for it was now possible to introduce English in an increasingly Canadianizing community. The ties with the homeland, which had been so strong in the early years, became more and more tenuous as both the immigrants and their children accommodated themselves to Canadian society. Cultural links to the Netherlands, never strong to begin with, now began to have less meaning. The old immigrants increasingly blended and integrated into Canadian society as no new waves of immigrants hindered their slow assimilation or adoption of Canadian ways. Like the Scandinavians in Canada, they so became a part of the society that they almost disappeared within it and lost their ethnic identity.

NOTES

1. Nieboer interview. Church bulletins of the period often commented on the problems of talking in church, smoking in church, and the control of children during the service. See P.J. Hoekstra Papers in the author's possession.
2. I am indebted to the Reverend Dr. J. Hielema and the Reverend Mr. T. Hoffman for insight and information on the developments in the Christian Reformed Church.
3. Interview with J. Heersink, October, 1972, Burlington, Ontario; J. Heersink, "The Canadian Work of the Reformed Church of America," John Heersink Papers.
4. Ver Hagen interview; interview with Ann Felix, March, 1980, Toronto.
5. Hielema interview. Information on the Christian schools in Canada received from Christian Schools International, Grand Rapids, Michigan.
6. St. Catharines interviews, 1972-75.
7. Ver Hagen interview.
8. For a survey history of the Reformed Church of America in Canada, see *The Church Herald*, 8 July 1977, pp. 6-13.
9. Interviews, Calgary, Alberta, 1977-80.
10. Institute for Christian Studies, "1980/82 Academic Bulletin" (1980), p. 5.
11. Interviews with the Reverend Mr. D. De Jong, Calgary, 1979-80.
12. Hielema interview.
13. The material contained in this section resulted from a series of formal and informal interviews that took place in Ontario, Alberta, British Columbia, and the Netherlands with Dutch immigrants and interested participants between 1972 and 1980. Their personal reminiscences and views provided an invaluable and penetrating understanding of the Dutch-Canadian community.
14. T.C. Van Kooten, *Living in a New Country* (1959), p. 157.
15. These figures are extracted from Oosterman, *To Find a Better Life*, p. 93.

NINE

The Community Today

The history of Dutch immigration to Canada spans the most active period of Canada's development as a nation. Yet the Dutch, while the sixth largest ethnic origin group in 1981, have maintained a relatively low profile in a country that prides itself on its multicultural composition and regards every ethnic group as a part of its cultural mosaic. Such a retiring position necessarily raises the question whether they have assimilated and disappeared or simply become invisible in the larger Canadian society. The answer is not a simple either/or but rather a combination of the two, and it is deeply influenced by the character of the immigration and the nature of the immigrants themselves.

The Dutch, unlike other Canadian ethnic groups such as the Ukrainians, Mennonites, or Vietnamese, were not forced from their homeland by political, religious, or social persecution. Largely lower or lower-middle class in social status, they were immigrants by choice rather than by duress and most came at a time of their own choosing, a time they regarded as optimum to their own advancement. The advancement they sought was economic independence and welfare, and Canada, of all the countries they had to choose from, seemed to promise the most in opportunity and growth.

They came also as relatively acceptable immigrants. The Canadians in recruiting them regarded them, above many others, as culturally adaptable and assimilable. Physically and socially they generally fitted the norms of Canadian society. In terms of labour they were immediately exploitable and a benefit to the developing nation. Similarly, from the Dutch point of view, Canadian society and Canadians, although different, had more to offer than mere economic advancement. A seemingly classless society, at least one based on wealth rather than birth, with European origins and founded on the work ethic, opened up new avenues of opportunity and even influence. Ideas and techniques from the immigrants' own experience were needed in Canada, and conditions there promised acceptance of the Dutch after a necessary period of economic and social apprenticeship or servitude. They were prepared to accept the Canadian promise of opportunity based on individual effort at face value until circumstances proved otherwise.

Such tempered acceptance from both sides, moderated by minimal anti-foreign prejudice toward the Dutch, at least compared to that which was directed to eastern Europeans and Asians by Canadians, permitted an easier integration and possible assimilation than was possible for other immigrants. It prevented the development of an antagonistic or protective or even nostalgic ethnicity that is so often the compensation for non-acceptance by the dominant society.

Another factor limiting the impact of the Dutch community has been its size in comparison to other ethnic groups. The 1981 census determined that the majority of the 408,235 Dutch Canadians lived in the provinces of Ontario (191,125), Alberta (65,060), and British Columbia (72,280) and that approximately two-thirds lived in the larger urban centres of these provinces. These concentrations clearly reflect the settlement patterns of pre-World War II immigrants and those areas designated by immigration officials as having the greatest economic potential. The result has been a scattering of the community across the breadth of Canada and a lack of physical cohesiveness.

Despite the high concentration in the urban centres of Canada, such concentrations are not easily identified by area or neighbourhood within those cities. Identification is easier in rural areas in and around such places as Truro, Nova Scotia, London, Ontario, Lethbridge, Alberta, and Abbotsford, British Columbia, where agricultural immigrants were in great demand at the time of their immigration and where they found land purchase relatively easy. While cities and urban areas may have greater concentrations of Dutch Canadians, the rural settlements are more ethnically prominent.

As for religious orientation, the census also indicated that 88,445 of the Dutch Canadians were Roman Catholic, 67,070 were Christian Reformed, 61,350 United Church of Canada, 44,240 of no professed religion, and the remainder adherents of other churches. Since the Roman Catholics and the United Church members (the majority no doubt drawn from the non-Calvinist Reformed churches of the Netherlands) can be regarded as members of non-ethnic churches, they have had little ethnic impact on the religious character of the Dutch community. Therefore, even though the Christian Reformed church members make up less than one-fifth of the Dutch-Canadian group, they have had an effect on the community out of all proportion to their membership. The reason lies in their solidarity and their identification as a "Dutch" church.

A serious question can also be raised about the actual size of the Dutch-Canadian community. The population figures as indicated by the census are probably not indicative of the true numbers. Many people who claim Dutch origin do so only on the basis of tenuous connections with Dutch ancestry many generations past. The Mennonites are the most obvious examples of such "genetic" Dutch Canadians. These people, however, have no real contacts or interest in the Dutch-Canadian community. It is estimated that between 1900 and 1970 some 200,000 Dutch immigrants came to Canada from the Netherlands or the United States. Even given the high birthrate the Dutch had before the 1950's, such an immigration could not have produced the presently claimed Dutch-Canadian population of 408,235. A conservative estimate would place the population somewhere between 300,000 and 330,000 Dutch Canadians.[1] This smaller number would help explain the low profile the Dutch have maintained in the general Canadian population.

THE DISAPPEARING LANGUAGE

The moment an immigrant ceases to think of his birthplace as "home" and begins to refer to it as the "old country," he makes a shift in thinking with important implications for his whole future life. The process of integration, which begins the moment he sets foot in the new land, demands new modes of thinking and action. The Dutch came with the intention of settling permanently in Canada and of seeking their fortunes. Most realized that the ties with the homeland inevitably would loosen. But it is fair to say that few considered the ultimate result of the action, that is, an alienation from their past. Many never realized that some of their most valued ideas and attitudes would undergo revision and challenge in the new society.

This revision was usually not a conscious change or redirection. It was not a matter of choice but something that happened due to circumstance and experience, a subtle moulding and accommodation that went unrecognized until it became blatantly obvious by exposure to new immigrants or by a visit to the old country. Few immigrants purposely abandoned the past or wholeheartedly accepted the Canadian way, yet by simply being in Canada they were changed. While most of the first generation never did become completely Canadianized, they also never remained wholly Dutch. They became transitional in character. Their children and grandchildren are Canadian and little of their origin remains to distinguish them from their fellow Canadian citizens. If the first-generation immigrants *integrated* into Canadian society and made their accommodation, then the following generations have *assimilated* and become Canadians.

One of the most important vehicles for retaining cultural identity among immigrant groups in Canada has been the use of their native language. Among Germans, Ukrainians, Poles, and others, language has helped to solidify and maintain ethnic boundaries, community solidarity, and differentiation from the surrounding communities. In these groups the value of language retention has always been, and continues to be, high. Yet among the Dutch this seems not to be the case. The study *Non-Official Languages* (1975) indicates that the desire for language retention among persons of Dutch origin is one of the lowest of any of the ten ethnic groups studied.[2] The reason for this is not clear, although it seems to be related directly to a value judgement on the part of the immigrants as to the usefulness of the Dutch language in their new homeland.

In the Netherlands, language has been both a divisive and unifying factor in creating a national state. The official language is Dutch. It is taught in all the schools and has been carefully standardized in all the provinces so that its teaching is uniform and complete. A second language is maintained in the province of Friesland, where it is still widely spoken in spite of the general use of Dutch. The retention of this language is due, in part, to the existence of a body of Friesian literature and a concerted effort on the part of nationalistic Friesians to maintain a cultural distinction between themselves and other citizens of the Netherlands. Past physical and economic isolation from the other provinces and perceived social and economic exploitation have helped to retain the use of the language.

Dutch immigrants to Canada carried with them the two languages. In the beginning years of settlement these distinctions began to disappear as standardized Dutch was the tool used to cross the language barrier. The use of Friesian was only continued within the family or among fellow immigrants from the same geographical area. Such use was also discouraged or minimized by the accepted belief that the use of dialect was a sign of either a lack of education or inconsiderateness. This view had been propagated in the Netherlands and a stigma was attached to the use of any language other than standardized Dutch.[3]

Prior to their departure from the Netherlands the immigrants were encouraged to take lessons in conversational English. Emigration societies and the Dutch government urged the necessity of fluency in the English language and stressed that integration was a desired condition, both economically and socially. Apparently few availed themselves of the opportunity to learn English and fewer yet were to discover any real connection between the British language taught at the English courses and the language spoken in Canada. On their arrival most had to come to terms with a new and often incomprehensible language.[4]

As a result, the first-generation immigrant created a new language, "Denglish." Those immigrants in their late thirties and older absorbed English words in their Dutch conversation and Dutch words in their English conversation, yet full fluency in English often escaped them. Immigrants with previous English education in the Netherlands were less susceptible to such mixing; the higher the level of education the easier it was to attain English-language fluency.

In 1975, a major national survey of first-generation immigrants found that 68 per cent still spoke Dutch fluently. The 32 per cent discrepancy is no doubt due to the inclusion in the sample of children of immigrants who accompanied their parents. Since there were no institutions for language maintenance in the Dutch community besides the family, and sometimes the church, their Dutch skills had rapidly diminished in the face of Canadian schooling and necessity. Fluency in the Dutch language for the first-generation immigrant children was also diminished by the parents' use of Denglish. Within a few years of settlement, it was clear that the retention of the Dutch language was often regarded as unnecessary.

In the second generation, the Canadian-born one, the rate of Dutch-language retention suffers a marked drop to 9.8 per cent. Yet the Dutch, among all the non-French or English-speaking groups, have the second highest percentage of people still having a fluent knowledge of the language. While this figure is surprisingly high, it is no doubt accounted for by the necessity to communicate with both the first generation and the relatives left in the Netherlands. Strong family ties and the ease of transport have meant that the connections have been strongly maintained. Some first-generation immigrants made a concerted effort to teach the language to their children so that their communication with *Opa* and *Oma*, *Tante* and *Oom*, could be maintained. While social and cultural values may have been surrendered in large measure, family relations have been maintained and can account, in some ways, for the continuance of the Dutch language.

Non-Official Languages indicates that the third generation has an even lower rate of retention than the second, those fluent in the Dutch language forming an almost negligible percentage (0.8). Yet, some knowledge of the Dutch language is retained, and again it seems to be related to the ongoing necessity of maintaining contacts with relatives overseas. One can assume that as these diminish, language retention will also further decline. By the fourth generation, Dutch Canadians will have few contacts with the old country and even less to distinguish themselves from other Canadians.

It is not hard to understand why fluency in the Dutch language has declined so drastically. Outside the family or among close friends the language is hardly ever used. Even within the family, Dutch is only used sometimes. Among fully fluent speakers it may be the main language of communication among family members but its use drops by half among friends. Each succeeding generation seems to follow this pattern, indicating clearly that use of Dutch diminishes the further one gets away from the first generation.[5] Since the family makes up only a small part of the social world, Dutch is appropriate for only a minuscule part of daily life. Lack of use leads to self-consciousness and to the reversion to the most familiar language, English. The maintenance of Friesian or dialect among certain individuals further minimizes the opportunity to speak Dutch.

While many of the first-generation immigrants find it easier to speak Dutch, their children and grandchildren find English easier. The first generation understands English, the children understand Dutch, and the resulting mixed conversation seems to bridge the communication gap. A handy bit of translation and a minimal understanding of Dutch suffices for the third generation. As death begins to take its toll among the first generation the babel of tongues is quieted and ceases to create any serious problems.

Since the Dutch-Canadian churches, credit unions, and social organizations have made a concerted effort to accommodate themselves to the English language they have not served any real function in retaining the Dutch language. The one exception seems to be the DUCA of Toronto, which has offered some Dutch-language instruction to its members and their children. The major Dutch-Canadian newspapers have been more successful in the continued use of Dutch, but even here time and the declining first-generation immigrant group, combined with Dutch-Canadian adaptability to English, have diminished their impact.

At the present time there are two exclusively Dutch newspapers being published in Canada with a combined circulation of some 10,000. The *Nederlandse Courant* and the *Hollandse Krant*, both published in Ontario, print Dutch news and commentary, views on Canadian events, editorials, advertisements, and regular columns. Their circulation has fallen with the decline in immigration and the loss of fluent Dutch subscribers.[6]

The two bilingual newspapers, *The Windmill Herald* (B.C.) and *Hollandia News* (Ont.), have a combined bi-monthly circulation of some 12,000 across the country. They offer relevant Dutch and Canadians news, news about Dutch Canadians, editorial perspectives on the Dutch-Canadian community, advertisements, and columns. Aware of the decline of Dutch readers they are making a concerted effort to become increasingly English and attempt to serve the needs of the growing English-speaking Dutch community in Canada.

The most successful Dutch-Canadian publication is the English weekly *Calvinist Contact* with a circulation of 11,000. Although it serves mainly as a church organ for the Christian Reformed Church and less as a newspaper, it reaches a considerable number of Dutch Canadians across the country. It keeps them regularly informed about events in the church and society and interprets these events from a "Reformed Christian" perspective.

A number of small church magazines are also regularly received by Dutch Canadians. *The Pioneer* (monthly) and the *Church Herald* (bi-monthly) serve the Reformed Church of America members. *The Banner* (weekly) and *De Wachter* (bi-monthly) are sent to members of the Christian Reformed Church, while the Canadian Reformed Church publishes the bi-monthly *Clarion* for its members. The Christian Reformed churches in Toronto and Edmonton also regularly publish newsletters detailing events in the churches in those communities.

Along with the newspapers and church magazines is the publication of books and material related to the churches and the Dutch-Canadian community. This need is filled by such Canadian publishing companies as Guardian, Knight, Paedeia Press, and Premier Printing. Although also working with general publications for the Canadian market, some have recently begun working on the publication of translated Dutch books and material related to the history of the Dutch in Canada. Other publications are directed primarily to the secular sector of the community. The DUCA *Post*, a monthly with 5,000 circulation, leads the innumerable clubs and society bulletins. These bulletins (usually mimeographed) provide news of club events, projects, and social occasions.

The majority of the publications that reach the Dutch-Canadian community are printed in English, recognizing the changing character of the constituency they serve. It is doubtful whether exclusively Dutch newspapers or magazines could now survive in Canada. Only a dramatic increase in immi-

119

gration from the Netherlands could put a halt to the process of Canadianization.

Although some attempt has been made to support Dutch-language retention in other media, the result has not been notably successful. Program time has been purchased on radio for Dutch programs but they have not been widely supported by the larger Dutch-Canadian community. Radio CHIN in Toronto broadcasts ninety minutes a day, with news, songs, and music from the Netherlands, but its audience seems to be largely limited to first-generation immigrants. The Dutch government supports the dissemination of its short-wave Dutch-language programs from *Radio Nederland*, but that audience also appears to be small. Some Dutch theatre groups exist across the country but their appeal is likewise increasingly diminished by declining audiences. Book IV of the *Report on Bilingualism and Biculturalism* suggests that "it seems most unlikely that the Dutch language will survive in Canada except as a language of immigrants."[7] Unless there is some significant resurgence of interest among third-generation Dutch Canadians, a resurgence stimulated perhaps by a search for historical roots, the Dutch language will soon be regarded as even more irrelevant than it is now.

There is, without doubt, a lack of concern among the majority of Dutch Canadians for the retention of the Dutch language. The immigrants were encouraged by government agencies, their churches, and their own desire for economic success to place little value on their native language. The institutions they created in Canada – the church, the credit union, and social organizations – were moulded, at least in regard to language, to the Canadian reality. The pragmatism that had dictated accommodation to the social and political diversity of the Netherlands was continued in the new land and positive results seemed to justify such a view. While a few might question the wisdom of abandoning the key to their native culture and a number of the second generation might make attempts to learn an almost forgotten language, the majority believed that if the price of success and achievement was the loss of the Dutch language then it had to be paid.

POLITICS AND SOCIAL CLUBS

As one of the larger ethnic groups in Canada, it could be expected that the Dutch would have a noticeable impact on the Canadian political process. This has not been the case. At the present time three members of the federal Parliament are of Dutch extraction (one senator and two members of the House of Commons). A number serve varying functions in the provincial governments, both in legislative and administrative capacities, and some are involved at the municipal government level. None of these are regarded as "Dutch" politicians, and they serve the interests of all the groups within their respective constituencies.

The lack of impact by the Dutch community in the political field has various origins. The fact that the majority of immigrants came in the post-World War II era has meant that they have been, in the main, too busy achieving economic independence to bother with politics. The struggle for financial security kept most of the first-generation immigrants from any active participation in community affairs. The difficulties of language made communication and involvement nearly impossible for a number of years.

Accustomed to proportional representation and politics based on ideology, the new Dutch Canadians found it hard to accept the winner-take-all philosophy of the Canadian system. To many, no real difference existed between the Liberal and Conservative parties. Both seemed motivated solely by the accumulation of power for power's sake. The orthodox Calvinists, who had passionately supported "anti-revolutionary" forces in the Netherlands, found liberalism of any degree or kind unpalatable. The socialist philosophy of the CCF was even worse, since it was regarded as basically humanistic and irreligious and therefore to be shunned. Such a view led many of this group to support the Social Credit Party both provincially and federally, for it seemed to give a nominal recognition to fundamental Christian beliefs.[8]

The essentially conservative nature of many Dutch-Canadian farmers and even city-dwellers manifested itself in a rejection of any party that favoured big government or statism. They had not left the highly bureaucratized Netherlands simply to reinstitute a government in Canada replete with forms, officials, and the squelching of individual initiative. The immigrants, predominantly of lower- or lower-middle-class origin in the Netherlands, were dedicated "to live the life of the solid middle-class man,"[9] and that meant the least government involvement possible in their daily lives and the least interference in their struggle for economic security.

Since the Dutch immigrants are not geographically concentrated, no one federal or provincial constituency has had a significant enough proportion to affect the outcome of an election. It is doubtful, given the division of the group along ideological lines, whether a Dutch-Canadian candidate could receive the wholehearted support of his own ethnic group.

It should also be noted that few other ethnic groups have had any real success in breaking into the Canadian power elite. In his study of the Canadian corporate elite, Wallace Clement notes that immigrants are generally excluded from the "opportunity structure." He claims that only by building parallel elites, as the Jewish Canadians have done, will ethnics be able to achieve the power and position now virtually controlled by the British and French charter groups. The Dutch have not established such a parallel elite and have therefore been unsuccessful in establishing a major presence in the superstructure of Canadian society.

The lack of ethnic homogeneity has also hindered the Dutch in speaking out with one voice that could attract the attention of other Canadians. While practically every city with any Dutch immigrants has a Dutch-Canadian Club, there is no national unifying organization to tie these clubs together. Occasionally provincial, federal, or local committees are organized to celebrate or remember some event of significance for Dutch Canadians, but these are temporary groups that disappear after the event. In 1967 a number of Dutch committees were organized to celebrate Canada's Centennial and the

Dutch contribution to it. Dutch carillons were given to a number of cities in Canada to express the immigrants' gratefulness for the benefits Canada had given them. In 1970 a committee collected money for an organ for the National Arts Theatre in Ottawa to celebrate the twenty-fifth anniversary of the liberation of the Netherlands. While these gifts have expressed a significant sentiment among Dutch Canadians, they have not led to any deeper ethnic identity, expression, or unity.[10]

The Dutch-Canadian clubs themselves are examples of the confusion and division that reigns in the Dutch community. Organized in the main by non-Calvinist Dutch, they have had limited appeal to the orthodox religious groups. Dances, card games, the consumption of alcohol, and theatrical entertainment have made such clubs unacceptable to a significant number of Dutch Canadians. While some did join to take advantage of organized charter flights to the old country or annual celebrations of St. Nicholas Day, they would not become involved in other social occasions or in the running of the clubs. Some of these organizations therefore have a short life span because they have to depend on a few people to do the work. While members of the larger Dutch community have become involved with specific projects, such as raising money for tulips for Ottawa or for the organ for the National Arts Centre, only a proportionately small group have remained as permanent contributing members.

In recent years, with stimulation from the federal government's multicultural program, Dutch-Canadian clubs have become involved in ethnic festivals such as those in Winnipeg, Toronto, and Calgary, but in reality these clubs only represent a small number of the members of the ethnic community. It appears that the social clubs are fairly successful in organizing events and supporting groups such as choirs and dancers, but as political pressure groups they have little power. Since they do not, and cannot, represent a broad spectrum of support within the Dutch community, because of its internal divisions, they are powerless to effect any significant changes within Canadian society. There is, furthermore, some doubt whether there are any changes the community sees as necessary.

Even within the clubs themselves, it would be difficult to achieve any significant solidarity because membership is not exclusively limited to Dutch Canadians. In many clubs, the proportion of non-Dutch Canadians has been steadily growing, either because of the intermarriage of Dutch Canadians with other Canadians or because of the active social life of the clubs, which pulls in members of the outside community. The ethnic alignment, while determining many of the social characteristics of the clubs, has not made them exclusive, nor is such exclusivity seen as necessary since the Canadian society seems to pose no danger to the Dutch community.[11]

Such an acceptance of the Canadian society lies partly in the fact that the Dutch, in large measure, have found acceptance by Canadians. The kind of overt prejudice experienced by eastern and southern European immigrants has not been experienced by the Dutch. As a result, they have not been driven back into themselves but have sought a larger place in the Canadian society.

Their basically pragmatic view, oriented by their middle-class desires, has emphasized the achievement of success at the expense of cultural traditions. The only exception, as we have seen, has been the retention by Reformed immigrants of their religious heritage, but even they have struggled to make this heritage relevant to the new environment.

The success of the post-war economic reconstruction in the Netherlands and Holland's continuation as a Western democratic country, free from Soviet oppression, have meant that nationalistic movements such as those seen among Ukrainian, Hungarian, or Polish Canadians have had no reason to develop. For Dutch Canadians, the question of loyalty has never been raised. They are Canadians first, with only vague and undefined connections with a readily accessible, if not well understood, foreign country.

CULTURAL REMNANTS AND MEMORIES

Faced with the process of integration and assimilation, many immigrants discarded aspects of their cultural identity that seemed irrelevant or inappropriate in the new Canadian society. There were, however, things of tradition or lasting value that were maintained and guarded, such as the Calvinist ideology. There were as well characteristics, ideas, and differences which, though less important, have differentiated them from other ethnic groups. Such cultural remnants and memories are some of the guideposts to the Dutch-Canadian identity.

For example, family names remain an important means of identification. Since they were generally not as unpronounceable to the Canadian tongue as some other foreign ones, the Dutch have generally chosen to keep them. English Canadians quickly recognized that a "van" (from), such as in Vander Berg, or a "de," as in De Groot or De Vries, connotes a Dutch name. Variations of "Boer" – de Boer, Boers, Boerman (from farmer) – also are familiar. There are, of course, many more names that are not so recognizably Dutch, such as Postuma, Postman, and Smit, but Canadians have never been loath to ask about ethnic origin, and an accent only encourages such an inquiry. Some immigrants did change their last names if such names were either unpronounceable or had sexual or derogatory connotations in English. First names such as Sjoerd and Wietzke were also often Canadianized, and many immigrant children simply took on Canadian equivalents for first names if their original names did not fit in. Children of immigrants have usually received Canadian names if they were born in this country. Although the general rule that dictated naming children after their grandparents was followed at first, this custom has begun to disappear. In recent years, the naming of children has been determined by popular Canadian fashion, while in some religious circles biblical names have made a resurgence.

In rural areas, Dutch farmsteads are sometimes marked by the names of the districts from which the immigrants came or by names of old country farms. Family names are prominently displayed on barns throughout the country and on many city dwellings. The fad to mark automobiles with the

123

country of origin of the driver has also led to the appearance of NL (Netherlands) bumper stickers on Canadian roads. Dutch provincial pride has even produced an occasional sticker from Friesland. The Dutch do not seem at all reluctant to display their origins in this fashion.

Another obvious sign of Dutch residency, visible to outsiders, is the continued use of the picture window valance or curtain. This curtain, the predominant fashion in the Netherlands, hangs across the top quarter of many Dutch-Canadian front windows. Made of figured lace, it has been retained by many first-generation immigrants, along with a profusion of houseplants, and is noticeable both in rural and urban areas. Its use by German immigrants and its abandonment, for more current Canadian styles, by second- and third-generation Dutch Canadians as "old-fashioned" now make the identification of Dutch homes somewhat more difficult.

Dutch businesses are often identifiable by the names of the proprietors (Voortman's Cookies) or the inclusion of the windmill logo or the use of "Dutch" in the name of the business itself. In Canada today, anything "Dutch" connotes cleanliness, hard work, and acceptability, and Dutch-Canadian businessmen take advantage of that association in their financial dealings with the general public. Most "Dutch" businesses could not exist without the patronage of Canadians outside the ethnic group. The only exception to this rule might be Dutch credit unions, whose membership remains predominantly Dutch.

Certain enterprises do, however, continue to cater to the ethnic community's needs. Although the Dutch language is less frequently spoken than before, such a service is usually available at Dutch bakeries, delicatessens, butchers, fish markets, and specialty stores that carry products to whet the appetites of the immigrants and their children. Bakeries make *bokkepotjes* (goats' feet); delicatessens carry croquettes, meat, and cheese; butchers produce Dutch cuts and *blinde vinken* (veal birds); fishmongers have smoked eel and mackerel; and the "Dutch Store" carries the familiar textiles, spices, and assorted other goods. Most of them also serve an increasing non-Dutch-Canadian clientele, which has adopted many of the Dutch specialties and products and made them part of their daily diet.

While Dutch foods and products are available to the general public and some supermarkets have "Dutch" or "ethnic" sections, the children of the immigrants have adapted themselves to the mixed North American cuisine. Hamburgers, pizza, casseroles, and other "Canadian" foods are more commonly served in the home than peculiarly ethnic foods. Good plain cooking of the North American variety dominates. Such foods as chicory, endive, kale, and broad beans, some imported from Holland, are an addition to the standard cookery, as are Dutch pastries and other sweets. Since the Dutch cuisine is made up basically of meat, potatoes, and vegetables it has little to distinguish it from the Canadian. Only Dutch restaurateurs serving Indonesian or French dishes have had any impact on the Canadian restaurant scene.

As far as alcoholic beverages are concerned, Dutch Canadians have in the past limited themselves in their selection. Canadian beer, although judged not as good as Dutch beer, has always been regarded as satisfactory and less costly than the imported variety. Canadian whisky quickly displaced *genever* (gin), although some might be returning to youthful tastes as it is now abundantly available. Since many of the Dutch were not wine drinkers at the time of their emigration, their consumption in this area has perhaps lagged behind. Specialty drinks of Dutch manufacture such as Advocaat and Curaçao are more readily available than in the past, but there is little evidence to suggest that Dutch Canadians consume more than anyone else. Moderate consumption of alcohol seems to be the general rule in the Dutch community, particularly in the orthodox circles. Restraint, not prohibition, is the determining factor; it is not uncommon to see alcoholic beverages served in homes after the Sunday morning church service. Alcoholism seems, however, to be no more common in the Dutch community than in the general public.

While the Dutch Canadians may be adapting themselves more and more to Canadian business practices and foods, they do preserve the family solidarity that was so important in the Netherlands and in their early years of settlement in Canada. Birthdays, baptisms, marriages, funerals, and ordinary Sunday get-togethers remain important in maintaining contact. Christmas, Thanksgiving, Mother's and Father's Day bring extended families, often from great distances, to the homes of family elders. Birthdays are seldom forgotten or uncelebrated and the visit of, or to, an old-country relative is generally a joyous occasion. Letter writing, whether overseas or to other places in Canada, although diminished by time, has been kept up. Telephone calls, even to the Netherlands, have helped to retain a certain family closeness, in spite of the great distances sometimes separating members. Many still preserve the time-honoured custom of keeping a birthday and events calendar in a convenient and prominent place, often the back of the bathroom door.

The close family ties in some ways have been a support in the increasingly unstable social conditions of the changing Canadian society. While the authoritarian and patriarchal nature of the family unit has mellowed over time, respect for parents and elders is still prominent. Many second- and third-generation children still go to parents and grandparents for help and advice and look to their personal relationships as models for their own. Even as democratic marriage relationships begin to predominate in the community, replacing authoritarian structures, many Reformed Dutch Canadians see value in the traditional value system that places the man at the head of the family. This and their religious orientation no doubt account for their low divorce rate.

Intermarriage has become more common as the differences between Dutch Canadians and their fellow citizens have begun to disappear. The second generation accepts the rightness and inevitability of choice outside the ethnic group, and the greater Canadianization of their parents makes such a choice acceptable. Only in more orthodox Calvinist groups has this tendency been opposed, and then only on religious grounds. National prejudices have, for the most part, disappeared. The result of such marriage has, of course, led to the sloughing off of any "Dutchness" that this generation may have retained, and most third-generation children have little awareness of their ethnic origin. Again, only in the Calvinist circles, due in large measure to the Christian schools, has some uniqueness been preserved.

The strong sense of family has also encouraged the Dutch to extend themselves in the community at large. As the children of the immigrants began to leave home, parents turned to fostering of children who were wards of provincial social agencies. Such care often led to the adoption of children who were regarded as difficult to place. Mixed race, emotionally disturbed, physically handicapped, and older children were accepted into the community. Social agencies found that the Dutch family provided a stable and loving home with fair and impartial discipline.

Orthodox Calvinists have regarded such social outreach as true Christian service to the Canadian society and have encouraged it at all levels. Given their religious orientation, they have attempted to set up social service organizations to deal with the clients' problems from a "Christian" perspective. Christian counselling services and organizations to treat the mentally ill and the handicapped have developed from this interest. The Christian Reformed community also supports a number of such agencies in the United States, including the Pine Rest mental health facility in Grand Rapids, Michigan, which is active in the treatment of depression-related problems.

The Reformed community has also supported local and world relief along with the Canadian churches. In 1979 and 1980, in response to the needs of the Vietnamese boat people, a number of Christian Reformed churches sponsored their immigration and settlement in Canada. They have provided homes, jobs, and language training and have attempted to help the refugees integrate into the Canadian society. Some churches now offer services in Vietnamese as well as English and Dutch.

As opportunities expanded in Canada in the 1960's and 1970's the Dutch immigrants, particularly in urban areas, began to take advantage of them both for themselves and for their children. Dutch-Canadian professionals made their appearance in the fields of education, engineering, medicine, law, architecture, business, and even the fine arts. There were few occupations they did not enter in or succeed at. As in the rest of Canadian society, women began to expand their role and leave behind the rigid patriarchal constraints that had inhibited them or their mothers in the Netherlands.

The scale of success measured against that of other Canadians exhibited no difference; in fact, except for their names, few could be identified as being peculiarly Dutch-Canadian. A few of the more prominent Dutch Canadians recently have been: Senator van Roggen of British Columbia; William (Bill Woodenshoe) Vander Zalm, the Premier of British Columbia; Debbie van Kiekebelt, the athlete; Aretha van Herk, the author; John de Visser, the photographer; Petra Burka, the skater; and the cookie kings, formerly of Mount Brydges, Ontario, the Voortmans. All were recognized for their individual accomplishments, not their ethnic backgrounds.

The record of Dutch-Canadian achievements is evident for those who know where to search, but where is the Dutch cultural imprint on Canadian society? What is peculiarly Dutch-Canadian about what the first and second generations have achieved? What has distinguished the efforts of this group from any other ethnic group that immigrated to Canada? With the exception of a few dance groups, choirs, or theatre groups, Dutch culture has made no impact on the Canadian scene. The question remains: what has grown out of the Dutch experience in Canada that is worth preserving, developing, and sharing with fellow Canadians? Perhaps it is too soon to ask that question; perhaps, too late.

While there is a small body of literature written by Dutch Canadians dealing with the immigration experience, it has been predominantly in Dutch. Only recently have writers begun to use English as a medium of expression. None has yet achieved any national prominence or notice, nor has a serious immigrant novel been written. Sociologists and other academics have merely scraped the surface in their examination of the group and as yet its characteristics lie largely undiscovered. The Dutch Canadian is, in great measure, the invisible ethnic.

As we have seen, invisibility was a matter of choice, not chance. Accommodation, integration, and even assimilation have been the desire of most immigrants and their children. Even though certain elements of "Dutchness" have been preserved, particularly among the first generation, these have not been seen to be in conflict with the dominant culture. Pragmatism has asserted itself in the keeping or discarding of things Dutch. Family loyalty and solidarity were seen as worthy of preservation, as were the doctrines and expressions of Dutch Calvinism. They were seen as ultimately being beneficial to the Canadian society even if, at times, they were in conflict with it. The preservers of such ideas are, however, in the minority as time goes by and they exert less influence on the larger group. The distinctiveness of the group, already minimal, becomes less and less as the Dutch Canadians cease to have an ethnic identity.

Some Dutch Canadians and even outside observers have expressed the hope that the more educated immigrants of the sixties and seventies would give voice and expression to the uniqueness of the Dutch experience in Canada. This has not been realized. While the Canadian Association for Netherlandic Studies has attempted to encourage the study of the Dutch role in the world and Canadian events, the larger Dutch community seems to have placed little value on its undertakings.

Presently, as economic growth and individual opportunity have become limited in an increasingly bureaucratized Netherlands, there has been a resurgence of interest in emigration. The newly arrived immigrants, however, blend in easily with the dominant society and, beyond social contacts, have little effect on the Dutch-Canadian community. As the culture of the Netherlands becomes increasingly North American, the differences between the immigrants and their hosts is reduced to one of language. Under such conditions the immigrant past is becoming a faded memory.

The past, however, is not lost; it is only silent. The immigrants of the early

127

post-war years are still alive, as are their memories. The joys, the sadness, the achievements, and the failures of their immigrant experience flavour their lives. Most of them have not assimilated; being neither wholly Dutch nor wholly Canadian, their integration has left them in a transitional stage. They have never completely abandoned the culture of their birth, nor have they completely accepted the culture of their adopted homeland.

The hopes and dreams of their youth were shattered by the harsh realities of existence. Canada became a focus for new dreams, and in some measure these were fulfilled. Yet every gain had its cost, and the immigrant experience exacted a price in loneliness, conflict, and anguish that made success a bittersweet thing. Most immigrants attempted to make a place for themselves in the new land, merging the unknown and the strange into the known, yet realizing that the fulfilment was less than the dream. Their loss has been tempered by their success and by a pragmatic acceptance that Canada is a consolation for what never could have been in the Netherlands.

NOTES

1. This statistical demographic assessment was prepared with the help of Dr. Helen Colbert.
2. K.E. O'Bryan, J.G. Reitz, O. Kuplowska, *Non-Official Languages; A Study in Canadian Multiculturalism* (Ottawa: The Secretary of State, 1975), p. 389.
3. Interviews, Calgary, Alberta, 1977-80.
4. Interviews, St. Catharines, Ontario, 1972-75.
5. O'Bryan *et al, Non-Official Languages*, pp. 128-30.
6. Interview, Albert vander Heide, Burnaby, B.C., May, 1980. Mr. vander Heide supplied the information and statistics on Dutch-Canadian newspapers and publications.
7. *Report of the Royal Commission on Bilingualism and Biculturalism*, Book IV, *The Other Ethnic Groups* (Ottawa, 1969), p. 135.
8. Interviews, Calgary, Alberta, 1977-80.
9. Joseph A. Diening, *Contributions of the Dutch to the Cultural Enrichment of Canada*, quoted in M. Boekelman, "Some Aspects of Dutch Post-World War II Immigration to Ontario," p. 5, unpublished ms. in the author's possession.
10. Interview, A. vander Heide.
11. The material relating to the Dutch clubs has been gathered by interviews in Calgary, Toronto, and St. Catharines. Some research has been done on the nature of Dutch-Canadian clubs by Cathy Cosgrove and has resulted in the unpublished manuscript, "Profile on the Dutch-Canadian Club of North Bay, 1978"; interview, Cathy Cosgrove, Toronto, February, 1980.

Bibliography

Aberson-Uges, J. *Van de Canadeesche Velden* (From the Canadian Fields). Groningen: Erven A. De Jager, 1934.

Brandis, Maxine. *Land For Our Sons*. London: Hurst & Blackett, 1955.

Breugelmans, Rene. "Dutch and Flemings in Canada," *Canadian Ethnic Studies*, 2, 2 (1970), pp. 83-115.

Broadfoot, Barry. *The Immigrant Years, 1945-1967*. Vancouver: Douglas & McIntyre, 1986.

Buurma, J.A. "The Adjustment Problems of the Netherlands Agricultural Immigrants in Canada," *Sociologisch Jaarboek* (The Hague, 1950).

Cavelaars, A.A.C. "Integration of a Group of Dutch Settlers in British Columbia," *International Migration*, 5, 1 (1967), pp. 38-45.

Cnossen, T. *Canada: Land van Vrijheit, Ruimte en Ontplooiing* (Canada: Land of Freedom, Space and Opportunity). Wageningen: N.V. Gebr. Zomer en Keunings Uitgeversmij, 1952.

Cook, Hugh. *Cracked Wheat*. Oakville: Mosaic Press, 1985.

Elliot, Una. "Comparative Roles of People of Italian and Netherlandish Origin in the Creation of a Homogeneous Population in the City of London," M.A. thesis, University of Western Ontario, 1964.

Francis, Robert J. "The Significance of American and Dutch Agricultural Settlement in Central British Columbia," Ph.D. dissertation, University of Minnesota, 1966.

Ganzevoort, Herman, ed. *A Dutch Homesteader on the Prairies* (Letters of Willem de Gelder). Toronto: University of Toronto Press, 1973.

——. "Dutch Immigration to Canada 1892-1940," Ph.D. dissertation, University of Toronto, 1975.

Ganzevoort, Herman, and Mark Boekelman, eds. *Dutch Immigration To North America*. Toronto: The Multicultural History Society of Ontario, 1983.

Ginn, Edith M. "Rural Dutch Immigrants in the Lower Fraser Valley," M.A. thesis, University of British Columbia, 1967.

Groenenberg, Adrian L. "The Social Geography of the Netherlands With Special Reference to the Role of the Church in the Integration Of Immigrants," M.A. thesis, University of Western Ontario, 1966.

Hartland, J.A.A. *De Geschiedenis Van De Nederlandsche Emigratie Tot De Tweede Wereldoorlog* (The History of the Netherlands Emigration up to the Second World War). Den Hague: Ministerie van Sociale Zaken en Volksgezondheid, 1959.

Hibbert, Joyce, ed. *The War Brides*. Toronto: Peter Martin Associates, 1978.

Hofman, Tymen. *The Strength of Their Years: The Story of a Pioneer Community*. St. Catharines: Knight Publishing, 1983.

Hofstede, Barend Peter. *Thwarted Exodus: Post-War Overseas Migration from the Netherlands*. 'S-Gravenhage: Martinus Nijhoff, 1964.

Lucas, Henry S. *Netherlanders in America*. Ann Arbor: University of Michigan Press, 1955.

Lowensteyn, J.H. "A Social History of the Dutch In Quebec," M.A. thesis, Concordia University, 1986.

Magee, Joan. *A Dutch Heritage*. Toronto: Dundurn Press, 1983.

Norel, K. *Hollanders in Canada*. Meppel: A. Roelofs van Goor, 1952.

Oosterman, G., *et al. To Find a Better Life: Aspects of Dutch Immigration to Canada and the United States 1920-1970*. Grand Rapids: The National Union of Christian Schools, 1975.

Palmer, Howard. *Land of the Second Chance*. Lethbridge: Lethbridge Herald, 1972.

Palmer, H. and T. "The Religious Ethic and the Spirit of Immigration: The Dutch in Alberta," in *Peoples of Alberta* (Saskatoon: Western Producer Prairie Books, 1985), pp. 143-73.

Paus-Jenssen, Arne Louis. "Immigration to Canada from The Netherlands, 1946 to 1963: An Economic Analysis," M.A. thesis, Queen's University, 1966.

Petersen, William. *Planned Migration: The Social Determinants of the Dutch-Canadian Movement*. Berkeley: University of California Press, 1955.

Rees-Powell, Allan Thomas. "Differentials in the Integration Process of Dutch and Italian Immigrants in Edmonton," M.S.W. thesis, University of Alberta, 1964.

Sas, Anthony. "Dutch Migration to and Settlement in Canada, 1945-1955," Ph.D. dissertation, Clark University, 1957.

Swierenga, Robert P. "Dutch," in *The Harvard Ethnic Encyclopedia*. Cambridge Mass.: Harvard University Press, 1980.

Tuinman, A.S. *Eenige aspecten van de hedendaagse migratie van Nederlanders naar Canada* (Some Aspects of the Present Migration of Netherlanders to Canada). 'S-Gravenhage: Staatsdrukkerij, 1952.

Vander Mey, Albert. *To All Our Children: The Story of Postwar Dutch Immigration to Canada*. Jordan Station, Ontario: Paideia Press, 1983.

Van Wezel, J. "Immigration from Holland and Land Settlement," in *Immigration and Land Settlement* (Ottawa: Canadian Catholic Conference, 1954), pp. 137-48.

Index

Agents: 9, 11, 13-15, 39-41, 53-54
Agricultural attaché: 68-71
American immigration policy: 36, 40, 64
Annapolis Valley: 27
Assimilation and integration: 23-25, 32, 42-43, 61, 81-82, 88, 94, 96-97, 102, 108-12, 114-20, 122-28

Banner, The: 100, 119
Boer, George: 15, 27

Calvin College: 108
Calvinism in Canada: 87, 100-01, 105-07, 121, 126
Calvinist Contact: 99, 119
Calvinist Emigration Society: 46, 49
Calvinist organizations: 100-01, 106
Canada Company: 54-55
Canadian immigration policy: 17-18, 35, 42, 50, 54, 67-68, 93
Canadian National Railways: 41, 51, 56
Canadian Netherlands Immigration Council: 71-72
Canadian Pacific Railway Company: 13-15, 18, 26-27, 39, 41, 46, 51, 56
Canadian Reformed Church: 101
Central Emigration Foundation Hol-

land: 41, 46, 48
Christian Emigration Central: 70
Christian Emigration Society: 9-10
Christian Reformed Church: 21-22, 24-26, 29, 47-50, 55-56, 70-71, 84-86, 96-102, 115
Christian schools: 95, 97-98
Church Herald: 119
Clarion: 119
Community divisions: 21-22, 25, 77-78, 85, 95, 97, 99-102
Compass: 99
Cox, Cornelius: 40
Credit unions: 105
Currency restrictions: 75, 79, 94

De Gelder, Willem: 15
De Jong, Klaas: 19-20
"Denglish": 117
Deportations: 52
De Wachter: 100, 119
Dewdney, Edgar: 17
Dignan, Father R.H.: 39
DUCA Post: 119
Dutch Americans: 8-9, 21-22, 24, 48-49
Dutch cleaning lady: 102-04
Dutch clubs: 21, 121-22
Dutch emigration policy: 8-9, 11-12, 15-16, 37, 40-41, 53, 56, 64, 66-67, 112

Education: 38, 43, 109-10, 126
Emigration fever: 65, 75
Emigration motivation: 5-8, 36-39, 62-66, 93-94

Fieldmen: 71, 78-80, 85, 89, 112
Free Christian Reformed Church: 101
Friesian: 9, 19, 117-18
Frijlink, Adjutant: 11

Geld-zucht (money lust): 108-09
Gritter, Rev. J.: 80

Haarlem Emigration Commission: 10
Hartland, J.A.: 67
Hoekstra, Rev. P.J.: 80
Hollandia News: 119
Holland Marsh: 53-56
Holland Reformed Immigrant Aid Society: 46, 48
Hollandse Krant: 119
Holtrighter, J.: 13
Homesteading: 12, 19-20, 29-31, 45
Hurgronje, J. Snouck: 67

Immigration Committee for Canada of the Christian Reformed Church: 70
Immigration Committee for Canada of the Reformed Church in America: 71
Immigration statistics: 36-37, 45, 50-51, 68, 72, 93, 112, 116
Insinger, Robert: 9-10

Juliana, Crown Princess: 61

Marriage: 107-08, 125-26
Maurer, J.: 12, 25-26, 29
Medical rejection: 75

Nederlandse Courant: 119
Neerlandia: 27, 29-31, 94
Netherlands Emigration Foundation: 51-54, 67-70
Netherlands Emigration League: 11-

12, 25-26, 29, 52
Netherlands Reformed Congregation: 101
Nobleford (Nieuw Nijverdal): 22-25, 94
Non-Official Languages: 116-18
Nordic: 17, 41-42
Nova Scotia: 27-29, 45, 51

Occupations: 31-32, 37, 40, 45-47, 82, 87, 89-90
Ontario: 12, 38-39, 46-48, 53-56, 87

Peddlers and entrepreneurs: 20, 90-92, 104-05
Pioneer: 99, 119
Placement system: 15, 40-41, 46, 78-80, 94
Politics: 120-21
Prins, Jacob: 56-57

Recruitment: 12-16, 18, 20, 24, 39-41, 46, 49, 53
Reformed Church of America in Canada: 25, 71, 86, 96, 99-100
Relief Land Settlement Agreement: 54-55
Religion and migration: 14, 20-22, 24-26, 29, 39-40, 42-43, 47-48, 56, 66, 69-71, 86-87
Roman Catholic Church: 40, 42-43, 70-71, 84, 86, 97, 99, 115
Roman Catholic Emigration Society: 40

Salvation Army: 11, 31
Schuurman, J.A.: 52, 54
Sifton, Clifford: 18
"Sin sheets": 86
Snor, John: 53-56
Social Action Department of the Catholic Immigration Aid Society: 70
Strathmore: 14, 27
Subsidies: 75, 95
Sunday labour: 106-07
"Swallow emigration": 38

Transportation loans: 10-11, 41
Troopships: 76-77
Tuinman, A.S.: 68

Unions: 100, 105-06

Van Aaken, Father: 14, 27
Van Ark, Willem: 30
Van Wezel, Father J.: 70
Ver Hagen, Father F.: 70

War brides: 64, 68

Washington, state of : 49
Windmill Herald: 119
Winnipeg: 19-22, 25-26, 31, 48, 94
Women and immigration: 37, 81, 102-04

Yorkton: 9, 19
Young Farmer's Program: 72

Zuilen: 69, 99